LONGFORD
FOLK
TALES

The
History
Press

Dedicated to the memory of my wife, Irene, who started the journey with me. To my lovely daughters, Joanne, Linda, Elaine and my buddy of a lifetime, Jack.

First published 2020

The History Press
The Mill, Brimscombe Port
Stroud, Gloucestershire, GL5 2QG
www.thehistorypress.co.uk

British Library Cataloguing in Publication Data.
A catalogue record for this book is available from the British Library.

ISBN 978 1 8458 8520 5

Typesetting and origination by Typo•glyphix, Burton-on-Trent
Printed and bound in Great Britain by TJ Books Limited

CONTENTS

Acknowledgements

Above all, I must thank the people of Longford. In researching this book, every door I knocked on was answered with a welcome and the offer of help. Thank you, Longford. Unfortunately, for every story included there were many more that had to be omitted. Co. Longford has enough folk tales to fill many volumes."

Dr Críostóir Mac Cárthaigh, archivist at the National Folklore Collection at University College Dublin, and the other staff in the UCD Folklore Department couldn't have been more helpful. The Main Manuscript Collection is huge and bewildering to a novice researcher. Their advice, help and guidance made the many visits to UCD a joy. Críostóir recognises that storytellers like to mould material to themselves. He prefers material to be left unchanged or changed as little as possible. I share his view. His support was a major contributing factor to this book.

Where appropriate, at the end of each story I have included references to the texts and material from the National Folklore Collection (NFC) as well as all other reference sources used.

The staff at History Press Ireland couldn't have been more helpful and understanding. When I started this book, the world was bright, and a new challenge was there to be both conquered and enjoyed. Unfortunately, life got in the way. The untimely passing of my wife, Irene, and my own personal medical issues that required two operations with slow rehabilitation have resulted in this project taking far longer than was reasonable. At no time since *Longford Folk Tales* was commissioned has anyone at HPI put any pressure on me to speed up its completion. Thank you all for your compassion.

Wherever possible I have tried to contact the copyright holders of any material used. If I have failed in this at any point I apologise and will correct any omissions in subsequent editions.

In acknowledging any group of individuals, gaps are inevitable. I have tried to mention all who helped but there are so many in so many ways that I'm sure I've not got everybody. To all who helped, offered help, named or omitted, all I can say is *mile buíochas.*

Specifically, I would like to thank Jude Flynn, a folklore institution in his own right. A man who is known in every parish and townland throughout the county. Jude's *Fireside Tales* is an annual publication that is eagerly awaited by all with an interest in Co. Longford and it's people; Mary Carleton Reynolds, County Librarian, and Martin Morris, County Archivist, always made me welcome in Library Headquarters. It became my 'base' but also a rabbit hole that I often willingly fell into, such is the richness of material in the archive.

Michael Masterson of Moyne, a man with a great sense of the past as demonstrated by his lovingly restored cottage. Michael introduced me to Micksey Mulligan, who taught me about horses, Goldsmith, Homer and life – a real privilege; Annette Corkery, Ardagh, who gave me 'The Wooing of Étain'; Hugh Farrell and all the members of Longford Historical Society, including the current Chairperson Camilla Kelly, for their network of contacts throughout the county; Noel Carberry at Corlea Trackway. Noel was the first person I spoke to when I started this journey; thanks Noel; Mattie Fox, Keenagh, who not only supplied me with his hospitality and local knowledge but with a tour of the whole area around Keenagh; John Casey, Lanesboro, for a view from the west of the county and much more besides; and James P. MacNerney, Dromard, for his kindness and a copy of *From the Well of St Patrick*.

Thank you, Joanne, for your meticulous correction of the final draft.

My thanks to fellow storyteller Steve Lally, who introduced me to the artist James Patrick Ryan, whose illustrations illuminate the text. James has a very distinctive style and a keen ability to find the kernel of each story on which to base his drawings. Having spent over a decade in China, his drawings have a Sino-Celtic style. Without James' essential help I would have been lost. Many thanks, James.

INTRODUCTION

Who owns a folk tale? Almost by definition it belongs to the 'everyman'. A story is never the same when told a second time, even by the same storyteller. That presents a problem when trying to attribute folk tales to their 'owners'. That great *seanchaí,* the late Eamonn Kelly, was asked by a fellow storyteller if he could borrow some of Eamonn's tales. Eamonn was very forthcoming in giving his permission but with one condition. The condition was that the storyteller would acknowledge from whom he had been given the story.

The provenance of a folk tale seems to me to be from whom it has been heard. The new 'teller' will make it their own anyway but in this way the roots of a story in the oral tradition can be passed on. In this book I have often used the Main Manuscript section of the National Folklore Collection. In all cases I have given as much information as I could find on the respondent (the storyteller) and where possible on how they came by the story. In this way it was possible to give the lineage of stories stretching back well in excess of a century and a half.

In some of the stories in this collection I have tried to get out of the way of the story and let it speak for itself. When the collectors for the National Folklore collection were out on the highways and byways collecting the treasure trove for the NFC, they would record the stories on wax drums using an Edison recording device. They would then transcribe their recordings verbatim – a challenging task to be sure.

In some of the stories here, I have, with the permission of Dr Mac Cárthaigh of UCD, used the same verbatim transcriptions. Sometimes this can make a story difficult to read but it allows the accent and dialect of the storyteller to come through. This is particularly true for example in the 'Stories of "Oney" Power'. Her stories were recorded and transcribed by Thomas McGrainne, and when they are read it's like listening to Oney herself across all those years. If you find them heavy going, stick with them, it will be worth it.

Folk tales are not history. However, real historical events give rise to folk tales that are passed down in the oral tradition. The resulting stories may add or change details (a good story never loses but gains as it is retold) but this does not matter. Real events, however distant, are the stuff of legends and if two versions differ, so what, they can both be enjoyed.

There is a lovely word used in North Co. Longford, *céilí*. This is not a dance as most people might interpret it but the visiting of neighbours for conversation, stories and craic. It is a word more associated with Ulster than with the other Provinces, 'Where is Pat tonight?' 'Oh, he's out on his *céilí*.' In other parts of the country this would often be called 'rambling'. In both cases it forms a very important part of storytelling and story gathering. It is the way stories are heard, enjoyed, perhaps modified and passed on to others.

Where I have referenced the Main Collection of the NFC, the references have been done by giving the volume number; page number(s); respondent's name; respondent's age; their address; the name of the collector and where possible the date collected. In some cases, the collector obtained further information about the provenance of the story. This I have included in the introduction to the story.

LONGFORD

DROMARD
BALLINAMUCK
DRUMLISH
GRANARD
NEWTOWNFORBES BALLINALEE
ABBEYLARA
KILLOE
CLONDRA LONGFORD
EDGEWORTHSTOWN
KILASHEE
ARDAGH
LANESBOROUGH
MOYDOW
CARRICKBOY
KENAGH
LEGAN
NEWTOWNCASHEL ABBEYSHRULE
BALLYMAHON

ABOUT LONGFORD

Co. Longford lies at the centre of Ireland. It is bounded to the north by Counties Cavan and Leitrim, to the east and south by Co. Westmeath and to the west by Co. Roscommon. It is the point where the three Provinces of Leinster, Ulster and Connaught meet. The original lands of the O'Farrell Clan were officially shired into the modern county in the late sixteenth century. The county of Longford is formed from the ancient lands of Annaly also known as 'Teathbha'. The name 'Longford' is an Anglicisation of the Irish 'Longphort', meaning a stronghold or fortress. The town of Longford from which the county takes its name was a stronghold of the O'Farrell Clan. The county crest is of a greyhound over a twin-towered castle. The motto is '*Daingean agus Dílis*', meaning 'strong and loyal'. The castle is usually taken to represent the long-phort of the O'Farrells.

Geographically the north of the county is hilly, being part of the drumlins that stretch across the north midlands. The southern parts are lower-lying raised bog land of better quality and more suited for tillage and grazing. Overall the county is low lying. The highest point is Cairn Hill (280m) near Drumlish, making the county the third-lowest in the country.

In the census of 1841, the county had a population of over 115,000. By 1886 that population had been decimated by famine and emigration to just over sixty thousand. Today the population has fallen further to approximately forty thousand. That makes it the second-least populated county in the country ahead of Co. Leitrim. A little-known fact relating to the emigration from the county relates to Edelmiro Julián Farrell, who was a former president of Argentina. He was born in 1887, the grandson of Matthew Farrell (1803–10), who had emigrated from Co. Longford. Edelmiro was linked to Juan Perón, who with his wife Eva succeeded Farrell to become president of Argentina in 1946.

1

Corn Hill, St Patrick, the Calleach and Furbaide Ferbend

Although Corn Hill, with a height of 280m, is the highest point of Co. Longford, it has the distinction of being the twelve hundredth highest mountain in Ireland. It is the third-lowest 'county top', with only Westmeath and Meath having lower high points.

Corn Hill is the modern popular name for the high point of Co. Longford. Despite its low summit, it was in the past possible to see nine counties from the top. Today, apart from a very unsightly television mast, the area is densely planted with Sitka spruce, which limit the view. Corn Hill is located between Drumlish and Ballinalee. The hill was also known as Cairn Hill or Sliabh Cairbré. In early mythological stories the hill is known as Sliabh Uillind.

St Patrick is very much associated with the hill. As is widely known, St Patrick travelled the length and breadth of Ireland, stopping at many places to preach the word of Christianity and to convert those he addressed. On his travels he came to the area of Corn Hill and stopped with a local chieftain. It was normal in such circumstances for the guest to be offered food and accommodation. Patrick was looking forward to a good meal as he was hungry from his travels. His meal was duly served. As soon as he tasted the meat, he realised that he had not been given lamb as he had been told but instead he was given dog meat.

The saint flew into the most terrible and unchristian-like rage because he realised that the meat he had been given was no accident but intended as an insult. It is dangerous to cross any saint, let alone St Patrick. According to the noted Irish scholar John O'Donovan, Patrick cursed all about him in no uncertain terms:

Accursed be Carbry's barren mountains
On which this hound was drest for me
Accursed its heaths, its streams and fountains
As long as man and time shall be
Accursed its glens, may no kind showers
Descend upon them from the skies
May neither herbs, nor grass nor flowers
Be ever seen in them to rise
Accursed its people, now I strike them
With my red bolt and seal their doom
May all good men for e'er dislike them
May they sink in murkiest gloom.

There are two cairns on top of Corn Hill. Two piles of stones that are the distinctive feature of the hill. These are no ordinary piles of stones, they are stones that are steeped in folklore and legend. The Pattern Day or 'climbing the hill' used to take place on the first Sunday in June. When this tradition was at its strongest, hundreds of people from the parish of Killoe and surrounding parishes would make the ritual climb. The tradition was for each climber to carry with them a stone that they would place on one of the cairns. This would bring the bearer luck but if a stone were taken from the cairn the result would be bad luck for the culprit. Sadly, this long-standing tradition is no more.

One of the cairns was originally formed by the infamous Calleach, or the divine hag, who was also the weather goddess. She ruled every winter from Samhainn (1 November) until

Bealtaine (1 May). As a deity she was possessed of many supernatural qualities. On one occasion she flew through the lands of Taffia, which Corn Hill divides. As she flew over the hill, she dropped a pile of stones from her apron. They landed on top of the hill and formed one of the cairns.

The second cairn has a more intriguing story. It is said to be the burial mound of Furbaide Ferbend. The story of Furbaide Ferbend comes from the Ulster Cycle of Irish Mythology. One of the central figures in this story is Queen Medb, Queen of Connaught and main protagonist in the Táin Bó Cúailnge.

Eochaid Feidlig became High King. He ruled for twelve years and died peacefully at Tara. Eochaid had three sons and three daughters. The daughters were Eithne, Medb and Clothru.

Eochaid married Medb to Conchobar Mac Nessa, King of Ulster. It was a bad marriage that didn't last very long. Eochaid then gave Conchobar another of his daughters, Eithne. They married and Eithne became pregnant. As Eithne's pregnancy developed she was warned by her wise man that there was a plan to kill her. She left and travelled west towards Cruachan, where she planned to have her baby.

As Eithne was now married to the Ulster king, Medb hated her as well. In her hatred and her wish to have revenge on Conchobar she arranged to have Eithne killed. Near Abbeyshrule, as Eithne was crossing the river rapids at Tenelick, she was confronted by Medb and one of her men. Eithne was drowned and as she died her baby was cut from her womb with the sword of the killer. It was a baby boy. This boy was Furbaide. Ever after this deed the river was named after Eithne – the River Inny.

At the age of seventeen, Furbaide fought in Conchobar's army at the Battle of Gáirech and later at the Battle of Ilgáirech, which came towards the end of the Táin Bó Cúailnge. It was said that he was so beautiful looking and fair that none of his enemies could bring themselves to wound him. Furbaide didn't have any such qualms about his enemies and slaughtered at least three hundred men in his opponent's army at the Battle of Ilgáirech.

As he matured his hatred of Queen Medb, his aunt, grew and festered. He knew he would have to avenge his mother who had died on the banks of the Inny. As she grew older, Medb often stayed on Inchcleraun an island in Lough Ree near Knockcroghery. It was Medb's habit to bathe at a certain well close to the shore of Inchcleraun. Furbaide learned that this was her habit anytime she was on the island. He hatched a plan to kill Medb and avenge his mother.

He took a rope and measured the distance from the well where Medb would bathe to the shore of Lough Ree. He returned to his home with the measuring rope and marked out the exact distance from shore to well. Having done this, he placed a stake into the ground at what would approximately be head height. On top of the stake he placed an apple. Day after day while his friends enjoyed life in feasting and play, Furbaide practised hitting the apple on the stake with a missile hurled from his sling. At first his efforts were very frustrating. Shots were either too high or too low, too far left or too far right. As the days of practice continued his misses became less. With each shot he was getting nearer and nearer the target. Eventually, he became so good in firing at that exact distance at a target at that exact height that he had to replace the apple with every shot. Now all he needed was opportunity.

As it happened, there was a great assembly called between the men of Connaught from the west and the men of Ulster from the north. The assembly was to be held around Lough Ree. One morning, as the Ulster men sat eating their breakfast, there was commotion among some of the men. Medb had retained her good looks as she aged.

'Look at the beautiful woman bathing on the island,' said one. 'Who is it?'

'That's Queen Medb of Connaught,' was the reply.

Furbaide scrambled to get his sling. This was the opportunity for which he had been waiting. While he had the sling, he had no ammunition. If he went to get a missile, Medb might be gone and the window of opportunity closed. He had been eating his breakfast and was holding a large lump of hard cheese. With necessity being the mother of invention, he loaded the sling with the cheese.

As he ran towards the shoreline, he began to swing the sling. Faster and faster it spun until by the time he reached the water's edge the sling and the cheese were just a speeding blur. He had just reached the water's edge when Medb on the island stood up and looked at what was happening. At this point she was at the exact height and exact distance that Furbaide had practised hitting for so many hours. He flung the hard cheese at Medb and hit her square on the temple. She fell to the ground, having been instantly killed by the blow.

Medb's body was recovered and she was taken to Knocknarea in Co. Sligo and there buried. They say she was buried in a standing position facing towards Ulster and her enemies. Lugaid came to avenge the death of Medb. He found Furbaide on the slopes of Sliab Ullenn (Corn Hill) and there killed him. The Dindshenchas says, 'A stone for every man that the axe clove – so was the cairn built: the king's son died in revenge for a woman: that is the origin of the Cairn.'

REFERENCES

'The Metrical Dindshenchas', Poem 10, ceLtucc.ie

'Corn Hill Cairns', visitinglongford.ie

'Slibh Chairbe', *Teathbha: Journal of the Longford Historical Society*, Vol. 1, p.1, 1969.

Celtic Literature Collective, www.maryjones.us/ctexts/medb.html

'The Tragic Death of Medb', www.headofdonnbo.wordpress.com/2016/04/19the-tragic-death-of-medb

'Memories of Derrycassin Wood', Derek Fanning, *Ireland's Own*, p.64.

A Brief Guide to Celtic Myths and Legends, Martyn Whittock, Constable & Robinson Ltd, 2013.

2

THE WOOING OF ÉTAÍN

The Yellow Book of Lecan, *written at the end of the fourteenth century, details the 'Wooing of* Étaín*' or 'Tochmarc* Étaíne*'. The story of* Étaín *and Midhir comes from the early Mythological Cycle with stories of the first people to come to Ireland in a series of invasions and is Co. Longford's greatest legend. This version was given to me by Sorcha Hegarty, who runs an annual Bard Summer School, and Annette Corkery of Ardagh.*

Midhir was a king of the Tuatha de Dannan, proud, handsome and regal. His wife was called Fuamnach and was his equal in every way. She too was tall and proud, and she was herself the daughter of a king. She was a good wife to Midhir, she looked after him, their children and foster children well.

One of these foster children was Aengus Óg, the God of Love. He was a lovely child and their favourite. Through the years they fell ever more in love with him – as you would expect with a love god. When he grew up, and moved away to his own home, they were bereft. Midhir especially missed him terribly.

One day, Midhir announced to Fuamnach that he was going to pay Aengus Óg a visit. On his way he met a very beautiful young lady. He stopped and asked her name. She told him it was Étaín and the moment she looked into his eyes, he fell in love with her and she with him. He asked her to come with him, and she readily agreed. The two of them then spent a year and a day at Aengus Óg's house at Brúgh na Boinne, living as husband and wife. Then Midhir decided that it was time for him to go home, but he could not bear to be parted from Étaín and so he brought her with him.

The moment Fuamnach saw Étaín she realised what had happened and she was furious. In secret she performed a magic spell on Étaín, transforming her into a pool of water. Then she conjured up a magic wind that dried up the water. The steam from the water condensed into a butterfly and only then was Fuamnach satisfied. However, the butterfly then flew to Midhir and wafted him with its wings. Beautiful music came up from the wings and a beautiful scent filled the air. Midhir recognised it was his love, Étaín. From then on everywhere he went the butterfly Étaín perched on his shoulder and the two of them were never seen apart.

Fuamnach was furious that her trick hadn't worked. She turned once more to magic and conjured up a storm. The storm caught Étaín and dragged her away from Midhir. She was blown and buffeted by the winds for many years, until at last the storm blew itself out and she found herself at Brúgh na Boínne, near the house of Aengus Óg. Aengus was able to recognise her and built a room of glass especially for her where she would be safe from any ill winds. He filled it with flowers and made it the most comfortable home for a butterfly that he could. Étaín lived there for some time until one day she mistakenly fluttered outside. Fuamnach's storm, which was always waiting, swept down and caught her up again.

The storm battered Étaín for seven long years and then it blew her in through the high window of a mortal king's banqueting hall. She landed on a rafter high in the roof. The king and his wife had laid on a feast for all their subjects. Exhausted, Étaín the butterfly fell in a faint off the rafter and landed in the wine cup of the king's wife. She drank back the butterfly and she turned to her husband and said, 'I am with child.' Nine months later she gave birth to a beautiful baby girl.

The king and his wife named the girl Étaín, and she grew up to be the loveliest young woman that anyone had ever seen, with no memory of her immortal life before.

Eochaid Airem, the High King of Ireland, was told by his advisors the time had come to find a wife. He heard rumours of this local king's beautiful daughter, Étaín, and decided that she should be the one for him. He called for Étaín to meet him and she was well pleased with the match. They married and lived happily together.

After some time, King Eochaid Airem's brother fell sick. On his sickbed, he called for Étaín, and when she came to him, he told her that he was lovesick because of the great love he had for her. He insisted that he would die if she would not agree to meet him in a love tryst the very next day. She agreed, and at once he felt better.

The next day, Étaín came to meet the king's brother at the arranged place, but as soon as she saw him, he changed form. He grew taller and a glorious light shone out of him. She realised that this was not her husband's brother. Indeed, it was Midhir, who told her the story of their love, and how he had been searching for her for three hundred years. Now that he had found her, after all the obstacles that they had overcome, he was never going to let her go again.

But Étaín was not convinced. She told him she knew none of this and had no memory of the things he was telling her, and besides all that, she was a married woman. Midhir called after her and said, 'If I get your husband's permission, will you come away with me?'

Étaín said, 'Yes,' thinking it unlikely.

The next day, Midhir turned up at the house of Eochaid Airem, and challenged him to a game of fidchell, a game not unlike chess. Eochaid Airem won the first game, and the second. He was so confident in his skills that he agreed to wager that the winner of the next game could claim any gift he asked from the loser. Midhir won and demanded that he be allowed to embrace and kiss the king's wife, Étaín.

Eochaid Airem was annoyed at this request. He certainly did not want another man to embrace and kiss his own wife. He therefore asked Midhir for a month's grace, and Midhir left, promising to come back and claim his prize.

Eochaid Airem readied all his army and spent the month training them and making sure they were fit, well-equipped and battle ready. On the day Midhir was to return, he ordered his army to the banqueting hall and to surround Étaín and prepared to repel any invader. But Midhir entered by magic and appeared inside the fort. He embraced Étaín and the moment he put his arms around her, she remembered everything. She remembered the storm. She remembered her immortal life. She remembered Midhir and their great love. She kissed him passionately, and as the king and all his men watched, Étaín began to shine with the light of the immortals. She and Midhir rose up from the ground and floated out of the window, never to be seen again. Eochaid Airem, broken-hearted, spent the rest of his life digging up every fairy fort he came across in search of his lost love.

REFERENCES

www.longfordtourism.ie/heritage/myths-and-legends/ midhir-and-Étaín

www.celtic-twilight.com/ireland/wooing-of-Étaín/index.htm

Annette Corkery, Ardagh.

Eriu, Vol. 12, ed. O. Bergin & R.I. Best, 1938.

Ancient Irish Tales, T.P. Cross & C.H. Slover, 1936 (Republished Barnes & Noble 1996).

3

LONGFORD AND THE *TITANIC*

The *Titanic*, or more accurately the sinking of the *Titanic*, is perhaps the most famous story in all maritime history. There were over 2,200 people aboard RMS *Titanic* under the command of Captain Edward Smith when it sank shortly after 2 a.m. on Monday, 15 April 1912. The sinking claimed the lives of more than fifteen hundred people. On first examination there may seem to be little connection between that terrible disaster in mid-Atlantic and landlocked Co. Longford, but there is.

Emigration since the Famine years (1845–50) saw approximately 61,500 leave the county between 1851 and 1911. In 1912, 426 people left the county and of these, fourteen were passengers on the ill-fated *Titanic*. All fourteen from Co. Longford were single and under the age of thirty. Their stories form part of the folk tales of the county from the early years of the twentieth century.

All of those from Longford were third-class or steerage passengers. There are many tales of third-class passengers being kept below decks and crew members using violence to stop the inadequate supply of lifeboats being overloaded.

The passengers from Co. Longford were:

David Charters, Ballinalee
Ellen Corr, Moyne
James Farrell, Killoe
Kate Gilnagh, Killoe
John Kiernan, Fostra, Aughnacliffe

Philip Kiernan, (John's brother)
Denis Lennon, Carrickedmond
Thomas McCormack, Ballinalee
Agnes McCoy, Ballinalee
Alice McCoy, (Agnes' sister)
Bernard McCoy, (Brother of Agnes and Alice)
Katie Mullen, Killoe
Kate Murphy, Aughnacliffe
Margaret Murphy, (Kate's sister)

Seven young men and seven young women setting off on the adventure of a lifetime. Ellen Corr, at sixteen years of age, was the youngest of the Longford passengers on the ship. So how did they fare? Did they die, or did they survive?

David Charters (21)

Before leaving home on his great adventure, David was telling his parents, William and Marianne, and his siblings about the huge size of the ship. He walked from his front door to a point up the field that was almost three hundred yards away. The entire family were incredulous that any ship that large and made of steel could float.

Sadly, David lost his life. His death was only the start of tragedies that beset the Charters family. One brother died as a child undergoing surgery. Another was killed in the First World War. A third brother was killed by the IRA in 1921 as they believed him to be an informer. Yet another brother died of a brain haemorrhage, while their sister Ann died while giving birth to her baby.

ELLEN CORR (16)

Ellen was emigrating to her two sisters, who were already established in New York or Jersey. Her father, who was a small farmer, at 65 years of age was very much older than his wife Bridget (44) when the sinking occurred. Ellen survived the tragedy. However, she never spoke of what she had experienced on the night of the disaster for the rest of her days.

She arrived safely in the United States and found work as a waitress. She later married an Irishman, Patrick Sweeney. They had no children and Ellen died on 9 March 1980. She was the last of the Longford survivors to pass away.

JAMES FARRELL (25)

James was one of the heroes of the disaster who failed to survive. His body was recovered still holding his rosary beads. He was buried at sea with little or no ceremony on 24 April. It was the policy aboard the ship searching for bodies in the days following the disaster not to recover bodies that were badly decomposed or crushed, especially if they 'looked like Steerage passengers'. This was in sharp contrast to the treatment of the corpses of first- and second-class passengers, many of whom were stored in ice and placed in funeral caskets.

Three other Longford travellers – Katie Gilnagh, Kate Mullins and Kate Murphy – found their escape route blocked by a crewman at a closed barrier.

> Suddenly steerage passenger Jim Farrell, a strapping Irishman from the girls' home county, barged up. 'Great God, man!' he roared. 'Open the gate and let the girls through!' It was a superb demonstration of sheer voice-power. To the girls' astonishment, the sailor meekly complied.
>
> Walter Lord, *A Night to Remember* (1978)

KATIE GILNAGH (17)

Katie was saved, saved because of a lie. When she managed to get to the boat deck, she was told that the lifeboat where she stood was too full. Katie started crying and shouted, 'But I want to go with my sister!' The sailor in charge had a change of heart and allowed her into the overcrowded boat, even though she had no sister aboard *Titanic*.

Katie's arrival at the lifeboat was only possible because of the gallantry of two men – James Farrell as described above and another unknown man on the second-class promenade deck. When Katie reached the promenade deck, she had no idea how to get higher to the boat deck. There was a man on the deserted deck standing beside the rail looking out sadly to sea but making no effort to save himself. He allowed Katie to stand on his shoulders and this way she managed to climb to the boat deck.

Katie Gilnagh was wearing a small shawl on her head as she boarded a lifeboat. The shawl blew away and James Farrell of Clonee took off his cap and gave it to her. As he did so he shouted, 'Goodbye forever,' and that was the last she saw of him.

About a week before the ship sailed a travelling woman had called to the Gilnagh household. Katie's father was turning the old woman away when Katie demanded that the gipsy read her fortune. She paid sixpence for the palm reading. The old woman told her that she would soon be crossing water and there would be danger, but that she would come to no harm.

Katie returned to Ireland in 1962 for the fiftieth anniversary of the tragedy. The flight to Ireland was only her second time crossing the Atlantic. On the flight the calm voice of the captain came over the intercom of the plane. 'Good afternoon ladies and gentlemen, this is Captain Smith …' Katie was immediately very upset and frightened. In fact, she had to be brought to the cockpit to make sure it wasn't the same Captain Smith who had been in charge of *Titanic*.

JOHN (25) AND PHILIP (22) KIERNAN

John had previously emigrated and had become established in New Jersey as a barman in premises owned by his uncle. He had returned to the family home in Aughnacliffe to bring his younger brother Philip to join him in America.

By all accounts, John was a very handsome young man and before emigrating he had begun courting a neighbour's daughter, Margaret Murphy. When he came home, Margaret had a plan of which John was unaware. She hoped to marry John and travel with him back to New Jersey.

On the night of his 'American Wake' party before returning to America, Margaret and her sister Kate attended. At the party Margaret finally told John of her plan. John 'reluctantly agreed' and also agreed that her sister could join them on the journey. Farrell may have been unaware that Margaret's family knew nothing of her plan.

It was brotherly love that cost John and Philip their lives. On their way up through the ship John called on Philip to go on, that he would be there in a minute. As they reached the stairs, Philip looked around and didn't see his brother and started back for him. This was the testimony of Thomas McCormack, a cousin of the Kiernans.

Slightly later, Margaret was trying to get to a lifeboat when John appeared on deck, shouted to her and came running up. 'Here, take my life belt,' he said. He made her put it on and that was the last she ever saw of him.

Both John and Philip Kiernan were lost. One of the strangest incidents following the tragic sinking relates to their parents. Before John and Philip left home for America, they made a solemn promise to their parents, John and Catherine, that no matter what happened they would come home. Both were drowned but in the early hours of the morning of the sinking and at approximately the very time of the sinking, the parents of the two boys heard the latch on the door of their home being opened. They saw both boys come in and go up the stairs to where they slept in the loft. Sadly, in the morning both beds were empty. Later when news of the disaster reached Longford the parents understood that their sons had kept their promise to return.

DENIS LENNON (20)

This is a love story from the sinking. Denis Lennon, Ballymahon and Mary Mullen (18) from Clarinbridge, Co. Galway, were eloping to America. Denis worked in Mullen's thriving pub and general store in Clarinbridge. Denis and Mary had fallen in love and planned to escape to the New World and start their lives together.

Mary was still a schoolgirl attending Loreto Abbey boarding school in Rathfarnham, Co. Dublin. She had gone home for the Easter holidays and was supposed to be returning to Dublin by train. As the train left Oranmore, Mary's sister, Bridget, said she thought she saw Lennon. The first indication that something was afoot was when the family received a telegram from the school saying that Mary had failed to return. Mary had indeed gone to Dublin but from there she took a train to Queenstown (Cobh) in the company of Lennon.

Mary's quick-tempered brother Joseph was a carter working in the Guinness brewery. He was also a heavy consumer of the same product! When Joe heard what had happened, he quickly put two and two together. He got a loaded gun and set out for Queenstown to shoot Denis Lennon, who had 'defiled' his little sister. However, when he arrived at Queenstown, *Titanic* had just set sail.

Both Denis and Mary were drowned. Joseph took to drinking in a big way and sadly drank himself to death. Her sister, Bridget, joined the Sisters of Charity.

AGNES (29), ALICE (26) AND BERNARD McCOY (23)

When *Titanic* started to get into trouble, the three siblings dressed quickly and made their way towards the boat deck about five decks above them. When they arrived there, they were told by an officer there was no immediate danger and they were to return below. They began to do as instructed but when Agnes saw water rushing into steerage quarters they stopped. By the time they got back to the officer the girls were just in time to secure a place. Bernard was left behind and watched as the boat was lowered.

They feared that Bernard had drowned. When they had been in the lifeboat for about thirty minutes, they saw Bernard in the water struggling towards the boat. When he grabbed on, he was beaten on the hands with an oar to make him let go. He held on and was then struck on the head and shoulders by the sailor. Agnes flew into a blind rage and attacked the sailor, throwing him to the bottom of the boat. In the meantime, Alice helped Bernard aboard.

All three survived. Agnes became a servant employed by the famous actor Douglas Fairbanks. Agnes never married. Alice was twice divorced and had another long-term partner. Bernard developed a permanent stutter from the trauma of that terrible night.

KATIE MULLEN (21)

Katie shared a stateroom on the ship with her neighbour, Katie Gilnagh, and with Margaret and Catherine Murphy from Killoe, Co. Longford. It was the actions of James Farrell recounted earlier that enabled Katie to make her way on deck. She was the last person to be taken on the lifeboat on which she made her escape. She survived.

Years later she told her own daughter that the last she saw of James 'was of him kneeling beside his suitcase saying the rosary'. When Farrell's body was later recovered, he was still holding the rosary beads.

Kate (17) and Margaret (19) Murphy

Kate and 'Maggie' ran away from home to join *Titanic*. Margaret left with the intention of marrying her neighbour, John Kiernan. The girls slipped away from home carrying all the clothes they could and went to the going away party at Kiernan's. There she told John she could not bear to wait while he got established in America and he reluctantly agreed to elope with her.

The girls' widowed mother, Maria, did not want her two daughters to leave her. She insisted they both stay on the farm and not abandon her. Margaret and Kate decided that they were going anyway. They hid their cases in the barn and began gradually smuggling clothes from the house to fill them. They did it this way, so their mother would not notice their packing.

Kate and Margaret both survived but, as already mentioned, John did not. Within two weeks of her arrival in New York, Kate met her future husband, Michael. In 1913, Margaret met Matthew O'Reilly from Cavan. O'Reilly was an undertaker and dance promoter. On their honeymoon they returned to Longford to make amends with her mother. Kate never returned to Ireland, having 'an extreme fear of water and flying'.

Another Longford resident who could well have been on that terrible list was James McGoldrick from Ennybegs, Killoe. Shortly before *Titanic* was due to sail from Queenstown (Cobh), James bought his third-class ticket for eight pounds and, like the others, prepared to make his way to the port to meet the great liner. However, two days before he was due to sail, he was unable to find his ticket.

He searched high up and low down, but no trace of the ticket could be found. In order to leave no stone unturned or any source of help untapped, he made his way to the church. There he asked the parish priest, Fr Tom Conefrey, to pray for divine intervention in his search for the errant ticket. Fr Conefrey told him to forget about the ticket and that all the hype about *Titanic* being the biggest ship in the world was just a publicity stunt. He told Tom there were many other ships crossing the Atlantic on which he could travel. Ominously he added, 'It may be all for luck that your ticket is missing.' James took the priest's advice and cancelled his passage.

How true Fr Conefrey's words were to prove. James McGoldrick eventually sailed from Queenstown on 27 April aboard RMS *Adriatic*. James was aged 30 at the time.

REFERENCES

A Night to Remember, Walter Lord, Holt McDougal, Reprint, 2008.

Fireside Tales, Jude Flynn, Vol. 11, 2013.

The Irish Aboard Titanic, Senan Molony, Mercier Press, 2012.

From the Well of St Patrick, Dromard Parish, p.161, James P. MacNerney, 2000.

www.encyclopedia-titanica.ord

www.irishamerica.com/2012/03/the-irish-on-the-titanic

www.longfordlibrary.ie/Heritage/Projects/Longford-The-Titanic

www.titanic.com/titanic_passengers_residing_county_longford_ireland.shtml

www.longfordlibrary.ie/Heritage/Projects/Longford-The-Titanic/Longford-the-Titanic-03-LongfordDead.pdf

www.longfordlibrary.ie/Heritage/Projects/Longford-The-Titanic/Longford-and-the-Titanic-Schools-Education-Pack.pdf

4

HUDDEN AND DUDDEN
AND DONAL O'NEILL

There are many versions of this story around the country. To the best of my knowledge the original was written by Joseph Jacobs (1854–1916), an Australian folklorist who popularised many of the most well-known English language fairy tales. His version of this story was published in Celtic Fairytales *(1892). The version here was told by John Reilly (80) a farmer from Drumhalry in Dromard parish. He heard it when he was 10 from Séan Davine (70), who also lived in Drumhalry.*

There were three farmers living in a townland in North Longford adjoining Drumhalry. They were very small farmers and lived next to each other. None were married and they all lived with their mothers. Their names were Hudden, Dudden and Donal O'Neill. Donal O'Neill was the cleverest of the three and he often played tricks on the others.

Hudden and Dudden eventually tired of O'Neill's practical jokes and after one particularly clever trick decided they'd had enough. Desperate situations require desperate measures and they planned between them to kill O'Neill. So, they set out to do the deed but by mistake they killed Donal's mother. Donal found his mother dead and after the initial shock he decided that he would have to bury her.

Donal's mother used to have a crutch, so he put her up on his back, held her crutch in his hand and set off to bury her in the graveyard attached to St Columcille's Parish Church in the townland of Aughnacliffe.

It was a very warm day and carrying the corpse of his mother was hot and thirsty work. When he reached Hourican's public house, he stopped to rest. Before he went into the pub, he propped his mother with her crutch against the well outside the pub. Then he went into Hourican's for a half-one. He told Micky Hourican, the publican, that his mother was outside and asked him to bring her out a half-one. 'She's a bit hard of hearing so you'll have to give her a shake,' said Donal.

The publican went out with the half-one and as instructed gave her a shake. First, she wobbled, then she fell down the well. Donal saw the corpse fall and ran from the pub yelling, 'Oh, me poor auld mother, you've killed her!'

'Never mind,' said Micky Hourican. 'I'll give you twenty pounds and say nothing about it. We'll bring her up and bury her.' This they did, and Donal got his twenty pounds.

There was a fair in Scrabby (also called Gowna) and Donal went to the fair and bought five calves with the twenty pounds. He was driving the calves on to his land when both Hudden and Dudden came down. 'Ah!' said Donal, 'you thought you killed me last night, but you killed my poor old mother instead. However, you did me a good turn. Look at the five fine beasts I've got. There's any money going now in town for old women's corpses. They grind down the bones and use them in the making of gunpowder! I got twenty pounds for my old mother and bought these calves in the fair of Scrabby.'

Hudden and Dudden were very surprised how events had turned out. Instead of getting rid of Donal they had set him up with five fine calves. There was a heated discussion between the pair of them and they decided that the best course of action was to kill and sell their own mothers while the market for dead old women was so strong. So Hudden and Dudden did just that. They killed their mothers, got each of them on their backs and went about the country shouting, 'Who will buy old women's bones for gunpowder?'

Naturally the police quickly heard that there were two men going around the country offering dead women's bones for sale. Hudden and Dudden were arrested, charged and convicted of the murder of their old mothers. They were each sentenced to seven years' transportation to Australia.

Now suddenly Donal had the use of all three farms – Hudden's, Dudden's and his own. He was very happy at the turn of events but knew there would be trouble when Hudden and Dudden returned from their transportation. He knew that seven years would be long enough for even those two to figure out how they had been duped.

They came back at the end of seven years with a lot of vengeance in their hearts. They made a leather sack and set out to catch Donal. It was a dark night and Donal was out lamping rabbits when they caught him and put him into the sack. They then placed the sack with Donal in it across an ass and headed off to Jack Masterson's. On the way a hare or rabbit jumped out of the hedge and went leaping down the road. Hudden and Dudden took the sack down off the ass and placed it on the ground before they went off after the hare.

Presently, there was a jobber from Ballinalee coming from a fair with sixteen head of cattle. As he came upon the leather sack, he could hear Donal singing 'God save Ireland said the hero'. The jobber stopped and asked Donal who was still inside the sack and where he was going.

'To heaven yeh boy yeh,' said Donal.

'What will it take for you to swap places with me?' asked the jobber.

'What will you give me?' asked Donal. 'I have sixteen head of cattle here,' said the jobber, 'and I'll give them to you.'

'Well loosen the cord and let me out,' said Donal. This the jobber did and got into the sack in place of Donal. Donal then tied the cord again.

'Now,' said Donal when he had the jobber securely in the sack, 'there will come two saints and lift you up to heaven, but you must stay very quiet and say nothing.'

This done, Donal went off with the sixteen cattle. The two 'saints' returned from their pursuit of the hare and put the sack with the jobber back on the ass. Off they went until they reached the Broken Bridge, where they threw him into the river and he was drowned.

The next morning Hudden and Dudden were more than a little surprised to not only see Donal alive but now he had sixteen fine head of cattle and he was driving them around showing them off to the whole world. Naturally they were wondering how he had got out of the sack but, equally important, where he had obtained so many fine beasts. They asked him, and Donal replied without a care in the world or even the slightest note of anger in his voice.

'When you threw me into the river yesterday and I sank down and I managed to get out of the sack there were hundreds of cattle down there. I only managed to get these sixteen because I was on my own and I had no one to help me get more.'

Hudden and Dudden asked Donal to tell them all about this wondrous place.

'Show us where you got the cattle,' said the two.

'I will,' said Donal.

So, the three of them headed off to the river where Donal had got the cattle and showed them exactly the deep pool where the cattle were. Hudden jumped in first, forgetting that he couldn't swim such was his greed to get cattle. Down he went but resurfaced moments later shouting, 'Hub-hub-hub, hub-hub-hub, hub-hub-hub!'

'What's he saying?' demanded Dudden.

'He wants help with the cattle,' said Donal. Dudden immediately jumped in, also forgetting that he too was unable to swim.

Hudden and Dudden both drowned and Donal got sole ownership of all three farms. He became a strong farmer after that for the rest of his life.

REFERENCES

NFC 1457, 2–6 John Reilly (80), farmer, Drumhalry, Dromard parish. He heard it when he was 10 from Séan Davine (70) Drumhalry.

Celtic Fairy Tales, Joseph Jacob, 1892 (Republished by Skyhorse Publishing, 2014).

5

The Stories of Nora 'Oney' Power

Nora Power was a traveller. She was known to one and all as 'Oney'.
She was born Nora Ward in Boyle, Co. Roscommon, in 1861 and
spent most of her life travelling in Connaught. She spent her later years
before she settled travelling the Longford/Westmeath border areas. She
was a natural storyteller, as were many members of the travelling com-
munity, especially in the first half of the twentieth century.

Pádraig Mac Gréine, one of the many great volunteer collectors
with the Folklore Society and later the Folklore Commission,
first met 'Oney' by chance. He came on her roadside camp as
he cycled through the Longford countryside at the village of
Ratharney, near Ballinalee. He put chat on her and asked if she
knew any stories. 'Oney' answered that, 'I could tell you stories
from this day to this day next week,' and indeed she could! Mac
Gréine noted that her stories flowed like water, she never missed
a word. She had a reputation for being able to tell and repeat the
same story over and over without ever changing a syllable.

She was a small woman and very thin. She had blue eyes and
was seldom in bad form. Pádraig described her as a 'very intelligent old woman and a fine storyteller'. He recorded her stories on
one of the three Edison recorders owned by the Folklore Society.
The Edison was a bulky machine weighing fifty-six pounds – the
portable recorder of its day. Recordings were made on fragile wax
cylinders and later transcribed verbatim by the collector. Collectors
were advised to write down the stories exactly as they sounded in
the vernacular. Reading these transcriptions can be challenging but

the reader is given as close a representation of how the storyteller sounded as is possible through the written word.

He recorded 'Oney's' stories on various occasions between 1930 and 1932. In her later years 'Oney' settled with her son, John, in Ballymahon. She died in 1937 in Ballymahon at the age of seventy-six. She was given an 'enormous funeral'. Her

family bought an expensive coffin and hired a hearse. However, they carried her coffin behind an empty hearse for almost two miles to the little graveyard of Cloncallow on the banks of the River Inny east of Ballymahon.

Jack the Irishman

Pádraig Mac Gréine took down this story from 'Oney' in September 1930. She was 70 at that time. In presenting it I have tried to stay faithful to the way in which Pádraig transcribed his recording of her story. However, I did have to make some slight changes to the phonetics used. I apologise to the memories of both Pádraig and 'Oney' for my blasphemy.

Once an' [and] once an' very good times, neither my time nor your time but 'twas somebody's time, when turkeys chewed tobacco an' swallows built their nests in ould men's beards there was a poor fisherman called Jack. There was no one but himself an' his wife, an' they were twenty years married an' had no children.

The fisnin' was very bad an' this day he was out in his little boat an' he had no luck at all. He never caught a thing. A merry-maid [mermaid] came up out o' the water an' says she to him, 'Yeh [you] have bad luck.'

'I have,' says he.

'Well,' says she, 'I'll give you the gift o' fish if yeh [you] promise me wan [one] thing.'

'I'll promise y'anything yeh like,' says he.

'Will yeh gimme [give me] yer eldest son when he's twenty-one?' says she.

'Bedad,' says he beginning to laugh, 'that's easy, for I'm married this twenty wan and has no childer [children].'

'Never mind that,' says she.

Off she went an' he began to fish. Sure in a few minutes he was tired pullin' fish into the boat. He rowed his little boat to the land an' went home with his fish an' told his wife all that passed. 'Ye'd never know what'd happen,' says she, referring to the possibility of a son. In nine months, she did have a son an' they called him Jack after his father.

When he was born, he was as big as a child of three an' when he was three, he was as big as a child of seven. He went to school an' he wasn't long there when he knew more nor [than] the master.

All this time the father had great luck at the fishin'. He got very rich sellin' fish in all the towns about. Wan day when the boy was near twenty wan, the father was out fishin' an' the merrymaid came up out of the water and reminded him of his promise. He had forgotten all about her, an' went home in very bad humour. He tould [told] his wife what had happened an' she began to roar an' cry an' lament for her darlin' boy. Young Jack came an' axed [asked] her what was up. The father told him all.

'Yeh have lots o' money now,' says he, 'so don't go near the wather any more, an' I'll go an seek me fortune.' His mother gave him a cake and a bottle o' milk an' he started out.

He thravelled [travelled] a long way an' he came to a big wood this day. He heard a terrible hullaballow goin' on an' he saw the Lion o' the Forest, the Hound o' the Forest and the Aigle [Eagle] o' the Forest fightin' over the carcass iv [of] a dead horse. 'Here's a man,' says the Lion, 'and he'll settle the dispute for us.' Did you know the animals could talk in them times? Jack went over to them an' axed them what was wrong. They told him they couldn't agree how to divide the carcass, an axed him to settle the dispute for them.

'That's aisy [easy],' says he, 'give the Aigle the tender bit, let the Hound take the hind quarters an' the coarse parts is good enough for the Lion, for he's well able to ate it.'

They were very thankful an' thanked him. Jack started off for himself again. He wasn't far gone when the Lion whistled after him. 'Bedad,' says Jack, 'I'm done now. Maybe they'll start dividin' my ould carcass the way I told them to divide the horse.'

He began to run an' they ran after him shoutin', 'We won't do anythin' to yeh. We want to give you a gift.'

Jack waited until they came up to him, an' says the Lion, 'I'll give yeh a gift that yeh can turn yerself into the Lion o' the Forest an' ye'll win over everythin' even the Lion o' the Rock.'

'I'll give yeh a gift,' says the Hound, 'that yeh can turn yerself into the Hound o' the Forest an' ye'll win over everythin' even the Hound of the Rock.'

'I'll gie [give] yeh a gift,' says the Aigle, 'that yeh can turn yerself into the Aigle o' the Forest an ye'll win over everythin' even the Aigle o' the Rock.'

Jack thanked them an' went about his business.

He wasn't far gone when he heard a hunt. 'What'll I do now?' says he to himself. 'Mebbe the dogs'll kill me if they catch me. I'll turn mesel into an aigle.' He was afraid to turn himself into any o' the lion or the hound. He was afraid the dogs of the hunt might catch him that way. He turned himself into an aigle an' flew away. He wasn't used to flyin' so where did he alight but on the breast of a horse.

There was a lovely girl on the horse an' she caught the aigle. She called her father for they were both at the end of the hunt an' says, 'Look at the lovely bird I caught. Come on an' we'll go home. We have enough for one day.' They went home an' she brought the bird home along with her.

That night when she went to bed, she brought the aigle up to her room with her. She blew out the candle and went to bed. When she did Jack says to himself, 'I think I'll turn back into meself and go look for somethin' to eat.'

The girl had only given him little bits and he was hungry. He turned back into himself and didn't the girl see him. She gave a screech but Jack tould [told] her not to be afraid. He up an' tould her the whole story about who he was an' all.

She thought she never saw such a nice lookin' fella an' she axed him to marry her. He said how could he face her father in the ould clothes he had on. 'But if yeh give me the price of a new suit of clothes,' says he, 'I'll come back an' ask yer father for yeh.'

She went an' gave him somethin' to eat and tould him she'd bring him out the next day an' he could go an' get the clothes.

The next day she brought him out in the form of the aigle an' when they got a bit away from the house, she hung a bag o' gold on his neck an' away he flew. When he flew away a bit, he turned back into himself an' walked into the town. He bought a lovely suit of clothes an' a gold watch and chain and a carriage and four [horses]. He got into the carriage and drove up to where the girl lived. 'Here's a grand driver comin',' says she to her father.

'Oh, bedad this must be some grand prince,' says he.

They welcomed Jack and got ready a grand feast.

'I'd like to marry that man,' says she.

'Shame on yeh,' says her father. 'How do yeh know but he's married already?'

'I'll ax [ask] him,' says she.

She did and Jack said that he wasn't and that's what had brought him there. He wanted to marry her. They all agreed, an' there was a grand wedding an' great faystin [feasting].

Wan [one] day after getting married they were walkin' along by the sea when up comes the merrymaid an' pilt [pulled] Jack into the sea. The poor girl ran home roarin' and cryin' an' tould her father. The father went off to the Grand Advisers and axed them how they'd get Jack back. The Grand Advisers told him for his daughter to go down to the seashore the next day and to jingle her three rings an' demand to see Jack's head over the water. The day after she was to go an' demand to see him to his hips an' the third day she was to demand to see him over the water altogether.

The next day she went down to the shore an' jingled her rings an' the merrymaid came up out of the water. The girl demanded to see her husband's head over the water. The merrymaid showed Jack's head an' the girl went away. The next mornin' she went down again an' jiggled her rings and demanded to see Jack to his hips. The merrymaid showed her Jack to his hips an' she went home. The third mornin' she went down an' said she would be satisfied if she saw Jack over the water.

The merrymaid showed him over the water. The minnit [minute] she did, didn't he turn himself into an aigle and flew away. The minnit he did, didn't the merrymaid grab the girl an' pulled her into the sea. Jack was in a terrible way an' went off an' told her father. He set off on the minnit to see the Grand Advisers.

The Grand Advisers told him that the Lion of the Forest would have to fight the Lion o' the Rock and kill him. They said that the Hound o' the Forest would have to fight the Hound o' the Rock and kill him. They also said that the Aigle o' the Forest would have to fight the Aigle o' the Rock an' kill him. When that was done Jack would have to take the egg that was in the Aigle o' the Rock and hit the merrymaid between the two eyes with it or he'd never get back his wife. The father went home an' told it all to Jack.

The next mornin' Jack went down to the seashore an' struck the big rock that was beside the sea with a sledgehammer an' out hops the Lion o' the Rock. Jack turned himself into the Lion o' the Forest, tore the throat out o' the Lion o' the Rock an' left him lyin' there dead.

The next day Jack came back again an' struck the rock with the sledge an' out came the Hound o' the Rock. Jack turned himself into the Hound o' the Forest and they began to fight. They fought all day an' inta the evenin'. Finally, the Hound of the Forest tore the neck out o' the Hound o' the Rock an' kilt [killed] him.

The next mornin' Jack came down early an' struck the rock with the sledge an' out came the Aigle o' the Rock. Jack turned himself into the Aigle o' the Forest. They began to fight. They fought all day an' inta the evenin' until the Aigle o' the Forest stuck his spurs into the Aigle o' the Rock and kilt it. Then Jack turned back into himself, took out his knife an' opened the aigle an' took the egg out of him.

He went home an' the next mornin' he went down to the say [sea]. The merrymaid was swimmin' around an' the girl beside her. The merrymaid was moaning to herself an' tossin' the girl's rings from one hand to the other. 'Jack,' says she, 'don't throw that egg at me an' I'll never interfere with yeh [you] any more.'

'Yeh mightn't interfere with me,' says Jack, 'but yeh might with someone else.'

He up with the egg an' hit her fair between the two eyes. The minnit he did, she turned into a heap of sand an' the girl was set free.

They went back home an' had great feasting for days an' days after.

REFERENCES

NFC 80, 182, Oney Power (70), Ballymahon, Co. Longford. Collector Pádraig Mac Gréine, September 1930.

NFC 1498, 1, Oney Power (71), Ballymahon, Co. Longford. Collector: Pádraig Mac Gréine, May 1932.

Irish Independent, C.O. Danachair, December 1978.

To Shorten the Road, George Gmelch & Ben Kroup, The O'Brien Press, 1978.

The Field Anthology of Irish Writing, Vol. IV, New York University Press, 2002.

NFC 80, 183–196, Oney Power (70), Ballymahon, Co. Longford. Collector Pádraig Mac Gréine, September 1930.

NFC 1498, 2–13, Oney Power (71), Ballymahon, Co. Longford. Collector Pádraig MacGréine, May 1932.

6

THE BLAKE MILLIONS

Urban legends make up a significant part of the folk tales of 'townies' in any county. This tale is regarded by many as being a semi-modern urban legend from Co. Longford. However, like so many legends there is often more than a grain of truth to be found. In this case it could be a very, very valuable grain of truth.

Often spoken about in North Longford are 'The Blake Millions', referring to a 'fortune' stored in a London bank just waiting to be claimed by their rightful owner. How did this fortune come about? Here is the story so far.

General Robert Dudley Blake was the son of General Sir Francis Blake, second baronet, of a very old and wealthy Northumberland family. They held the family 'pile' at Teissel Castle near Durham. While he was a captain in the army, Robert Dudley Blake met a beautiful young Irish girl from Longford named Helen Sheridan in Dublin. Helen was the daughter of a country schoolmaster. In some accounts, however, she is described as a 'servant girl'. Blake provided for her education to be completed in England. He married her in Lanarkshire in 1819. Their only child died in infancy and Blake having quarrelled with all his relations shortly after the marriage, left his entire estate to Helen when he died in 1860. In the same year his brother, Sir Francis Blake, third baronet, died without legitimate issue and the baronetcy became extinct. Sir Francis also left considerable property to his sister-in-law, Mrs Helen Blake.

Did Sir Francis marry his sister-in-law before his death? There is no record of a marriage certificate but given that Sir Francis left all to Helen suggests that there was most likely a union between them. Further, with the fact that Helen was granted probate of the estate, it is a safe assumption that they had married.

Helen died at 4 Earlscourt Terrace, Kensington, Middlesex, in 1876 at the age of seventy-six without making a will. There are wildly varying estimates of her real and personal estate values, but all remained in the hands of the Crown. Advertisements were placed looking for people with legitimate claims to all or part of the estate. Naturally there were many false claims, including one that involved General Blake's solicitor and clerk. It was alleged that these gentlemen had destroyed original documents in their possession and substituted them with false ones. The charges were proven, and both received jail sentences.

In 1900 an American nun who had heard of the story came to Ireland looking for Sheridans in Co. Longford. This lady had a cousin who was a Sheridan among the many Sheridans of North Longford. At that time there were Sheridans in Dromard,

Legga, Drumhalry, Corrinagh, Enaghan, Crott, Rossduff, Moyne, Aughakine and Carrickmaguirk. The nun also travelled to London. As she could show no proof that she was connected, she got no help from the authorities. She also tried to establish the value of the estate. The estimates that were circulating at the time ranged from thousands to millions. She was a very persistent lady and finally the administrators hinted that the value was £300,000. This was a huge sum at the time. Consider the value today with the addition of compound interest and we really are talking about millions.

The Irish Party in Parliament tried to prevent the British Treasury taking possession of the estate but by 1905 their attempts had failed. There were many claims to the fortune from England, Ireland, the United States and Australia. However, to date none have satisfied the Court of Chancery of their bona fides.

In 1909 the *Tuam Herald* of Saturday, 14 August reported that a Mr Fred Blake had died also intestate and it was believed that he was a distant relative of the original Blake fortune. His estate, although not as large as the main hoard, was added to the pot.

So, if you are a Sheridan and have any connections with North Longford get out the family tree and you just might find that you are in for a 'windfall'. You should be warned than none have been successful to date despite lots of efforts made. However, there is always a first, and it could be you!

REFERENCES

Tuam Herald, 14 August 1909.
www.genealogy.com/forum/surnames/topics/Sheridan/2605
The Register (Adelaide, South Australia), Tuesday, 29 May 1928.
The Mail (Adelaide, South Australia), Saturday, 9 January 1932.
Fireside Tales, No. 3, 2005, p.24, Jude Flynn & Lizzie Sheridan.

7

PHELY REILLY AND THE FAIRY FORT

This story was given to folklore collector James Delaney by John Mulligan, a 77-year-old farmer from Dunbeggan, in the parish of Columkille. The story is almost identical to the 'Legend of Knockgrafton' documented by Thomas Crofton Croker in Fairy Legends and Traditions *in 1825. The main difference is that in Croker's version the days of the week are in Irish and the story is located near Cahir, Co. Tipperary.*

There is a fairy fort in the townland of Birrinagh, Killoe, and one night Phely Reilly was coming home and heard music, dancing and singing coming from the fort. He looked over the ditch and there he saw little men and women and they were all singing. They were singing, 'Monday, Tuesday, Wednesday,' then they would add, 'Thursday, Friday,' over and over. Phely was listening for a while and when the fairies sang, 'Thursday, Friday,' Phely sang out, 'and Saturday.'

The fairies stopped singing and shouted out, 'Who's that?'

'It's Phely,' said one of them.

'Bring him here,' said the fairies, and Phely was brought before the King of the Fairies.

'What did you interrupt us for?' asked the king.

'You were singing the days of the week and you weren't saying them all, so I finished them,' answered Phely.

'Is there another one?' said the king. 'We never knew that.' He turned to the fairy crowd and said, 'What will we do to Phely for giving us that information?'

One of the fairies answered, 'He has a hump and we could take the hump off him.'

Phely did indeed have a terrible hump on his back. 'Send for the doctor,' ordered the king.

Soon the doctor came and cut the hump off Phely. Phely went home in great good humour and told everybody what had happened.

There was another lad we'll call Jack living not far from Phely and he also had a hump that was as bad or even worse on his back. When he heard what had happened to Phely he decided he too would make his way to the Birrinagh Fort.

Jack did just that and when he heard the fairies sing, 'Monday, Tuesday, Wednesday,' and then, 'Thursday, Friday, Saturday,' he shouted out, 'Sunday!'

'Who's that?' shouted the fairies. 'Bring him in.'

He was brought before the King of the Fairies, who demanded, 'What do you mean by spoiling our song?'

'You were leaving a day out,' said Jack 'and I put it in.'

'You're a liar,' said the king. 'Sunday is not a day of the week, it's a day of rest.'

'What will we do with him?' the king asked the fairy crowd.

'Put another hump on him,' shouted all the fairies.

This was done, and Jack went home with two humps on him for the rest of his days.

References

NFC 1457, 533–534, John Mulligan (77), Farmer, Dunbeggan, Granard, Co. Longford. Collector James Delaney.

Fairy Legends and Traditions (1825), Forgotten Books, republished 2007.

8

Co. Longford Wake Games

The games below are as told by Frank McNaboe (73), who was a miller and small farmer living in Rossduff, Columcille, near Granard. The most striking aspect of the games is the level of physical 'punishment' that was dished out to participants during them. It is easy to understand their potential for triggering fights that were so often part of wakes. Not all games were as aggressive as those below. Other games included card games, tests of strengths, hide and seek games and guessing games. As many wakes lasted several days and nights, those present had to find ways to pass the time, and more importantly, to stay awake during the long hours of darkness.

The Nine Daughters

This was a matchmaking game. It was a simplified variant of 'Old Dowd and his Daughters', described by Kennedy in *Banks of the Boro: A Chronicle of the County of Wexford*. One man, who was the 'father' of nine marriageable daughters, was the principal in this

game. Someone in the crowd who didn't know the game was chosen. This dupe was to act as the suitor for one of the daughters' hand. He approached the father of the nine daughters and said when asked his business, 'I want a wife.'

The father replied: 'My nine daughters are all down by my knee and no folly tinker will get one from me.'

The next thing the father asked the suitor was did he want much money with his daughter. The suitor told the amount of the dowry required and the father replied that he couldn't pay all the money down in a lump sum but that he would pay the suitor in gales (a 'gale day' is a day on which rent or interest was due). At this juncture a couple of fellows caught the suitor and lifted him over the arms of two other men. These latter two faced each other clasping each other's hand (the right hand of one clasping the left hand of the other) with arms outstretched. The unfortunate suitor was placed face down over these outstretched arms and for every instalment or gale that the father had to pay, someone gave the suitor a prod of a big pin in the backside. So, the more money the suitor asked, the harder the treatment he got.

PUTTING THE HOG TO BED

Four were necessary to play this game. One fellow, who we'll call the leader, had a big rope with knots in it. This was to drive the hog. Two other fellows stood in the middle of the floor with their arms around one another. Then some of the others in the room caught some victim and put him on his hands and knees in between the legs of the two standing with their arms around each other. One of these two caught the 'hog' (the fellow on his hands and knees) with his legs around the hog's neck and so he had him in a tight grip. The second fellow standing gripped the hog around the hips with his knees. They then had him so that he could not stir. The leader, with his knotted rope, gave the 'hog' a good beating with it. Then they caught someone else and did the same to him and so on.

HOLD THE LIGHT

This was played with a lighted candle. Someone was chosen to stand in the middle of the floor. The others, as many as could manage, stood around him. One eye of the chosen one was blindfolded and the other was partially blinded by holding a lighted candle in front of it. Then one of those standing around slapped the blindfolded man with a leather strap and the blindfolded man had to say who it was that had slapped him. What they did was, they took the candle away from his eye and those that were standing began to run around him in a circle. The partially blindfolded man had to name the person who had struck him. If he couldn't name, the person that had struck him the game went on again. He was blindfolded as before and someone struck him again on his outstretched hand. All the best hitters would get around him and hit him with the strap.

He had to take three turns or guesses. If he could guess who had struck him that person then had to take his place. If at the end of the third round he had not guessed correctly then he had to select another man, called 'a foul man'. When he had been blindfolded three times, he had the right to name a successor to take his place.

TOSSING THE HERRING

This game was played by one person at a time. It was a balancing feat. Two chairs were necessary. They were placed facing each other and a strong stick, like the handle of a shovel or a hay fork, was placed between them with the stick resting on the seat of each chair. Two clods (sods of earth) were placed on each chair, one on each side of the stick ends. The player then sat 'tailor wise' on the stick and helped to balance himself with the aid of a walking stick. He had to use this walking stick to knock off the clods (or 'toss the herrings') off the chair. It was comparatively easy to knock the clod off the chair facing the player without losing balance. The difficulty arose when he had to knock the clod off the chair behind him, as the rules of the game compelled him to pass the stick under his legs at the knees. The inevitable result was, of course, that he fell before knocking off the clod behind. He was then given a severe 'thump'.

One of the conditions of the game was that you had to place the walking stick in the right hand to knock off (or toss) the left-hand clod and then change the stick to the left hand to knock off the right-hand clod. In some places the player was allowed the use of two walking sticks, one in either hand.

Kissing the Stirrup

This game was similar to the previous one in that two chairs and a stick were rigged up as in 'Tossing the Herring'. Instead of the players sitting tailor wise on the stick, however, two belts were obtained, and these were placed on the stick with the buckles uppermost. Two men in the company would supply the belts. These belts then hung down from the stick like stirrups. However, they didn't touch the ground. The player had to stand with a foot in each 'stirrup' and the only thing he had to balance himself was the stick to which the 'stirrups' were fixed. Even this would be a difficult feat, but then the player, once he was balanced in the stirrups, had to try and kiss the stick. What usually happened was that when the player tried to kiss the stick, the effort of bending down caused his feet to shoot out and up and he found himself falling on the ground, which he met rather severely. As Frank McNabo said, 'The stirrups went from under you and your backside hit the ground.'

Who Has the Button?

Any number of people could play this game. The players sat around in a circle and the leader of the game got a button or some other small object. With this in his cupped hands he went around the circle of players, each of whom held out their hands similarly cupped. The leader dropped the button into some player's hands. He then asked one of the other players, 'Who has the button?' If the player guessed correctly, he himself became the leader of the game and the first leader had to sit down in the successful one's place. If the player failed to guess who had the button, he got a slap of a leather strap. The leader then asked some other player.

THE PRIEST OF THE PARISH

Any number of players could also play this game. They all sat around in a circle and the leader began, 'The priest of the parish has lost his "considering" cap. Some say this, and some say that, but I say my man John.'

The player named as 'my man John' then answered, 'Who said you, sir?'

Leader: 'Yes, sir, you sir.'

Player: 'Not me sir,' and then he named another player. The leader of the game then named another player. The leader of the game then repeated this player's name already mentioned by the first player. This dialogue was carried on at as fast a pace as possible. If the player whose name was thus mentioned failed to answer his name immediately it was mentioned, the leader beat him with a stick.

Frank McNaboe said the players used their own names. In some other parts of the country, for example Wexford, the players were given a name to which they were to answer. The dialogue was carried on so rapidly that it often happened that a player would not be prompt enough in answering his name and so was beaten.

SHUFFLE THE BROGUE

The players sat around in a circle on the ground with a man standing in the centre. This man was often chosen by lot. The players had an old slipper or sometimes a knotted rope. The players sat with their legs drawn in towards their bodies and the knees sticking up. They placed both hands underneath their legs and sat very close together, so that they could pass the 'brogue', the slipper or the rope to one another, without the player in the middle being able to see who had the 'brogue'. The standing player then went from one sitting player to another searching for the 'brogue'. If he found it with a player, that player in whose possession it was found had to stand in the middle and the first standing player sat down in his place.

The fun of the game was that as the player was on one side looking for the 'brogue', the 'brogue' would be in the possession of some player at the opposite side. The player possessing the rope or 'brogue' took advantage of the other player's back being turned and hit him as hard as he could on the backside as he stooped down to search for the 'brogue'. As the player struck the man searching for the 'brogue', he shouted out, 'Hoola, harra, shuff, shuff, shuff.' Then he'd 'shuff' it away from him, i.e. he'd quickly get rid of the 'brogue' by passing it to either of the players on his right or left. This game was also called 'Hush Horra'.

REFERENCES

NFC 1399, 514–522, Frank McNaboe (73), Rossduff, Co. Longford. Collector: Jim Delaney.

The Banks of the Boro, A Chronicle of the County of Wexford, Patrick Kennedy, McGleshant & Gill, Dublin, 1875 (Republished by Hard Press, 2017).

NFCS 0751, 430, Patrick Casey, Ardoghil, Co. Longford, Sr M. Clement, Ballymahon, Co. Longford.

9

Co. Longford Ghosts

Every county in the country has its own share of stories of the para-normal. Here is a selection from The O'Farrell Country. *Wherever possible the provenance of the story has been included. Many of the stories are based on items in the wonderful series* Fireside Tales *produced every year by Jude Flynn of Longford Town.*

The Drumlish Devil

This story comes from Thomas Vaughan, Derryharrow, who in turn heard it from the late Nertney Brothers.

In the mid-1890s the people of Longford were rightly proud of the opening of the magnificent St Mel's Cathedral in Longford town. Religious fervour was running high throughout the county.

There was a family living at the time in Cloonmacart townland, not far from Drumlish. Against the more usual flow of emigration to the United States, a member of this family who had worked most of his life in the US returned home.

The initial joy of the returning relative quickly evaporated when the family realised that this man had given up his religion and no longer went to Mass nor received the Sacraments. The family tried everything they could to get him to return to his faith. Neither persuasion nor coercion had any effect. He had giving up on the Church and that was that.

He had returned to his native country to retire and live out his days around Drumlish, the town of his childhood. His enjoyment didn't last very long. He became ill and it was clear that his days on earth were numbered. This only made the family more distressed that he might die without receiving the last sacraments and be damned as a result.

One night the man's condition deteriorated rapidly, and the family knew that the hour of his death was at hand. Fr Tom Conefrey was sent for to come to the house. Fr Conefrey, like the good man he was, could be depended on at any hour day or night to tend to a member of his flock, whether they be inside or outside the fold.

Around midnight, the sound of the priest's horse could be heard galloping up Clonmacart Lane. The family looked out the window and saw the horse just outside the house abruptly stop, rear up and snort in fear. Fr Conefrey calmed his mount and tied it to the wheel of the cart outside.

The priest here came in with his usual, 'God Bless all here', with the family answering, 'and the same to you'.

Without delay, Fr Conefrey made his way upstairs to the sick room, telling the family to remain downstairs. At first the family were taken aback at being excluded but it was clear from the priest's tone that it was an order, not a request.

As soon as the priest entered the room of the dying man, all those gathered downstairs heard Fr Conefrey shout in a stern voice, 'As quick as I came, you are here before me.'

Who was he talking to? The family believed it was to the Devil who had come to get the Yank's soul. They then heard the priest say with great conviction, 'I'll settle you me bucko when I get this candle lit. I have no fear of you or your likes.'

In these times people believed there were two things that the Devil couldn't fight against and that was Holy Water and a lit blessed candle. It was for this reason that every family kept both items in their homes.

The priest prayed over the dying man for a long time. Eventually he came down and said, 'Ye needn't worry about him any more, he's ready to meet his God.'

The family were much relieved that their relative had received the last sacrament as he was dying. They thanked Fr Conefrey for his good works but one of them asked, 'Who were you shouting at when you first went up?'

The priest looked at the questioner eye to eye and said, 'I spoke to no one other than prayed to God for that man's soul.'

He didn't bat an eyelid as he answered. Ever after that the family were convinced that Fr Conefrey had squared up to the Devil in the room and through his faith drove him from the house so that the dying man could pass in peace.

The Longford Dog

Pádraig Mac Gréine, the great folklorist, related this story. There was a man called Sheridan who lived near Drumlish on the side of Corn Hill. When Sheridan was a boy, he had a great friend, as most lads do as they are growing. The two were inseparable, they went everywhere together and did everything together.

Sadly, without warning Sheridan's best friend died. The boys were inseparable not only in life but in death. The boy's ghost began to appear and the two, boy and ghost, continued to hunt and sport together. As well as remaining his best friend, the ghost protected the Sheridans' crops and prevented any would-be robber of their turf.

Problems began, however, when the ghost began to socialise with the young Sheridan. At night when Sheridan went céilíing (visiting) with his neighbours he was openly accompanied by the spirit. One night he was in this certain house playing cards when two women from the house went out to the haggard to fetch turf. The spirit went with them but would not allow them to fill the basket no matter how they tried. In frustration the women returned to the house and demanded that Sheridan put manners on his spectral friend and let them get on with their work.

Sheridan went outside and confronted his friend, the ghost. 'I want you to leave here now and come home,' the ghost said with a note of urgency. Sheridan refused as he was playing cards well that night and the luck was running with him. The spirit disappeared in frustration. Sheridan returned to the card table. When he went back there was a large black dog under the table. There had been no dog there earlier.

Nobody else in the company saw any dog but Sheridan and it glared at him with teeth bared and emitting a low growl. It had fiery yellow eyes and smooth black furry coat. Suddenly, Sheridan realised why the ghost of his friend wanted him to leave and fear knotted his stomach. This could only be the pooka or similar manifestation.

The atmosphere in the whole house had become tense since Sheridan had returned to the table. The players were bad tempered and there was little fun to be had. The players and even those not involved in the cards began arguing over the slightest thing. It was only a matter of time before matters got out of hand. Two brothers accused each other of cheating. One word begot another and before long they began to fight. As they tussled on the floor the older brother managed to grab a heavy poker that was lying in the hearth and struck his sibling a killing blow.

A stunned silence fell on the house as the older brother stood with the 'weapon' in his hand, tears flowing down his cheeks. The coroner put the incident down to 'death by misadventure' but the family ever after blamed Sheridan and his ghost for the dispute that had led to the death. People around the area began to avoid him. He was no longer welcome to go céilíing at any house in the area.

Sheridan knew that the only way he could redeem himself within his community was to get rid of the ghost. The spirit was aware of what Sheridan wanted to do. One night the ghost said, 'Whatever you do, don't get rid of me between the froth and the water.'

It wasn't clear to Sheridan what his other worldly friend meant but he kept away from all rivers, streams and lakes. Eventually Sheridan told his companion it was time and that he must go. The ghost simply nodded, and Sheridan buried him under a bush near his home. Ever after that bush was known as 'The Pooka Bush' and Sheridan was slowly accepted back into his community.

THE KILGLASS GHOST

This story was told by Mr and Mrs Brendan Kenny, Kilglass, Legan, Co. Longford. They had heard the story from Ambrose Taylor, who was sexton at the Church of Ireland, Kilglass.

During the First World War the Rev. William Lee was rector of the parish. He had a son, Irwin, who joined the British Army, as so many young men did at that time. Irwin was home on leave for Christmas 1915 when, shortly after the festive season, he received a telegram telling him to report in all haste to Richmond Barracks in Dublin to re-join the 10th Royal Dublin Fusiliers, in which he held the rank of sergeant. Normally the Rev. Lee and his wife would take Irwin by horse and trap to the railway station in Edgeworthstown and wait to see him off as the train pulled out from the station.

On this occasion Irwin was so anxious to answer the call of duty he didn't wait for his father to make ready the trap but grabbed his bicycle and headed at great speed towards the station, with only a quick kiss for his mother and handshake for his father. His parents were broken-hearted at not having been able to say goodbye properly before he departed.

During late April 1916, Rev. William Lee was conducting his normal Sunday 3 p.m. service. During the service all his congregation heard the sound of hobnailed boots marching up the aisle of the church. After the service the rector told the sexton Ambrose Taylor that he wished to see him in his study in the rectory immediately. When the two men were alone, the Rev. Lee asked Ambrose if he had seen or heard anything during the service. Ambrose said that he had heard the sounds of boots, as had all the congregation. Rev. Lee was clearly very shaken because he said that not only had he heard the steps but had seen a man in khaki uniform and pith helmet walking up the church.

The following day the Lee's received a telegram informing them that their son, Sergeant Irwin Lee, had been killed in the Dardanelles at the disastrous landings of 25 April in Gallipoli. Irwin was nineteen years of age. There is a plaque to his memory in the Church of Ireland, Edgeworthstown.

The Headless Horseman of Granard

In 1886 J.P. Farrell described the British garrison in Granard as being 'the most ungovernable corps in the British service'. The officer in charge of the garrison was a Captain Blundell, described as being 'the cream of the service … in dress, manners, sporting propensities and general recklessness.'

One night there was a large social function held in the officers' mess, where all the young ladies were invited for an evening of music and dance. Blundell, as was his fashion, charmed the ladies throughout the evening. At the daily parade the following morning Blundell failed to appear on parade. This was most unusual as he was noted for being punctual. 'Play hard and soldier hard' was his motto. By lunchtime there was still no sign of the officer in charge. His colleagues wondered if he had perhaps escorted one of the young ladies home after the ball was over, or perhaps he'd had too much to drink. The latter possibility was most unlikely as Blundell was known as a man who could 'hold his drink'.

One of his fellow officers went to his room to see if in fact Blundell had overslept. The door was locked and despite his banging on the door there was no sound of his captain inside. The junior officer then called more of his fellows and they checked Blundell's window. It was closed and locked securely. The decision was taken to break into the officer's room.

When they managed to gain entry, a terrible sight met their eyes. Blundell was lying in a heap behind the door while his severed head stared at them with sightless eyes from under the bed. It was obvious he had been murdered as suicide was an impossibility. The difficulty was that both door and window had both been securely locked from the inside.

The answer was never discovered. Since then many, many people around Granard have claimed to have seen an apparition of the headless Blundell riding a black horse through the town around midnight.

The Ghost Priest

This tale is from Mrs Eugene Reilly from Corrickmaguirk in the parish of Columcille. Mrs Reilly was forty-five years old when this tale was given to Jim Delaney. Mrs Reilly didn't know Jack's surname and said all she ever knew him by was 'Jack'.

Jack was fond of rambling and the priest was always after him. The priest kept telling him that he'd come to no good because of his ways. One evening Jack went to the cobbler to collect shoes that were being mended. The shoes hadn't been repaired so Jack decided to wait for them to be done. The cobbler told him they would be hardly done that night.

Jack complained, saying the cobbler had promised they would be ready and ready they would be even if he had to wait until midnight. 'Don't you know there's the ghost of a priest sitting at midnight on that bridge you have to pass on your way home.' The cobbler told him to go home and that he would have the shoes completed for sure by the following night. 'Priest or no priest, I'm not going home without me shoes and I'll wait for them.'

So, Jack céilíed till two o'clock in the morning, when he eventually got his boots and set off for home. He got as far as the bridge and saw the figure of a ghostly priest sitting on it. He hesitated. He was afraid to go on but ashamed to go back, especially as the cobbler had given such a clear warning. Finally, he decided to go ahead and chance it. On he went till he came to the bridge with a priest sitting on it. It was the late Fr Morris.

'Good night Father,' said Jack.

'Good man Jack,' said the ghost priest. 'Now that you have spoken to me, you'll have to help me. I want you to come with me to your own priest.'

This was the priest who was always scolding Jack. Jack said that he would go, even though he didn't like the idea of going to the priest at that time of night.

When they came to the river, the ghost priest said to Jack, 'You'll have to take my hand here.' (According to belief among the people, a ghost can't cross water, a river or a stream.) Jack took the hand and it felt like rough wood. They continued on and eventually came to the priest's house.

Jack knocked hard on the door and after some time an upstairs window opened and a sleepy looking priest stuck his head out and demanded in a harsh tone, 'Who's that?'

Jack said it was him and that he had Fr Morris with him.

'Go home, you blaggard,' said the priest. 'You're drunk, that priest is long dead.'

The ghost of Fr Morris said to Jack, 'If he doesn't believe you, tell him that you know that we were both ordained on the same day, you first and Fr Morris after you.'

Jack repeated the words as instructed and the priest hesitated before answering, 'Wait there and I'll come down.' This he did, then the living and the dead priest got engrossed in conversation while Jack stood by waiting for them to finish.

When they were finished talking, the dead Fr Morris said to Jack, 'Now Jack, you'll have to bring me back to the bridge and then with God's help I'll be able to go straight to heaven.'

They headed back the road for the bridge and eventually came to the river. The ghost priest stopped and reminded Jack that he would have to take his hand to enable him to cross the water.

This time the dead priest's hand was soft and smooth, just like a glove. They crossed the river and continued on towards the bridge. Jack could see that the ghost priest seemed radiant, happier and lighter in himself. Jack knew that indeed the dead priest was about to go to heaven.

'Father do you think have I ever a chance of going to heaven like you?' asked Jack.

'Well Jack,' said the priest, 'it's the heart that gains heaven and you have a good heart despite all your rambling.'

Jack was a bit embarrassed at this statement and cast his gaze down towards the ground. This was just as they arrived at the bridge. Jack looked up and Fr Morris had disappeared.

REFERENCES

Fireside Tales, Vol. 1, Jude Flynn, 2003.

Irish Ghost Stories, pp.140–142, Padraic O'Farrell, Gill & Macmillan, 2004.

Real Irish Ghost Stories, pp.70–71, 81–82, Paul Fennell, Currach Press, 2009.

Fireside Tales, Vol. 4, Jude Flynn, Longford, 2006.

NFC 1457, 384–387, Mrs Eugene Reilly (nee MacNaboe) (45), Corrickmaguirk, Berinagh, Columcille, Co. Longford, Jim Delaney.

10

HE STOOPS TO CONQUER

Oliver Goldsmith was not a physically attractive man but all of society wanted his company. He was born in 1728 in a rundown farmhouse in Pallas, near Ballymahon, Co. Longford. His father, the Rev. Charles Goldsmith, was the Church of Ireland vicar of Forgney Church. The reverend both farmed and attended his clerical duties to support his large family of seven children. Shortly after Oliver was born, his father was promoted to the rectory of Kilkenny West, Co. Westmeath. This post had a salary of £200 per annum and a decent house. The Goldsmiths' living standards improved a little.

When Oliver was six, he contracted smallpox, which left him scarred for life. This was very unfortunate because he was considered unattractive even without the ravishes of smallpox. An early tutor described him as 'never so dull a boy; he seemed impenetrably stupid.' These are not the sort of opinions to generate confidence and self-belief. It was compounded further at the diocesan school of Elphin, where despite being regarded as kind, affectionate, cheerful and agreeable he was described as 'a stupid, heavy blockhead, little better than a fool, whom everyone made fun of'. He was shy, reticent, small and awkward in stature and heavily bullied. As he grew, he became much less shy and more arrogant.

Although the family had left Co. Longford in 1730, young Oliver was to return in 1741. He was sent to school in Edgeworthstown as a pupil of Rev. Mr Hughes, who conducted a classical school in the town. On one infamous occasion, as a rather gauche young man, Goldsmith was riding at the end of his summer holidays from his home at Lissoy to school in Edgeworthstown. He was enjoying the freedom of the road on an old nag of a horse, with a guinea in his pocket and a twenty-five-mile journey ahead. Goldsmith, who could never manage his finances, felt the money burn a hole in his pocket. He got as far as Ardagh, when night overtook him, and he decided to find an inn for the night. He demanded directions from one of the locals to 'the best inn in the neighbourhood'. Although originally shy, Goldsmith had developed an approach that seemed arrogant. It was his misfortune or luck depending on one's perspective that the person he asked for directions was a local trickster called Cornelius Kelly.

Kelly took great pleasure in directing the self-important young man not to an inn but to Ardagh House, home of the Fetherstone family. Literally on his 'high-horse', the young Oliver rode off to the 'best inn'. When he arrived at the front door he walked straight past the butler and demanded food and a room for the night.

Baron Thomas Fetherston recognised him as the son of his good friend the Reverend Charles Goldsmith and decided to play along. Goldsmith was rude and arrogant to the 'staff', in reality, the entire Fetherston family. It was said that one of Fetherston's

daughters took a fancy to the young Oliver, who treated her as a common serving wench. Naturally he demanded the best room at the 'inn', which he was given.

The following morning, he called for the bill, still in

a demanding fashion. He still assumed that Lord Fetherstone was the 'inn keeper', only to be told that he had 'never kept an inn' and that he was in fact a good friend of Goldsmith's father. He further added to the young man's embarrassment by telling him that there would be no charge for eating, board nor lodgings, and that he was a welcome guest of Lord Fetherston. This must have been one of those moments when the individual in question wished that 'the ground would open up and swallow him'.

It was clear to Master Goldsmith that news of his adventure would reach his father before he did. It did. This story was confirmed in a letter written by Goldsmith's sister, Catherine. The upside of this social disaster was that the event provided the basis for Goldsmith's famous play *She Stoops to Conquer* (1773), which is one of the few eighteenth-century plays still being performed today. The 'she' in the play is Miss Fetherstone, who 'stooped' to become a maid in her own home.

Goldsmith lived only a short life, passing away in 1774. His life was haunted by excess and debt. Before he died, he had run up outstanding debts of £2,000, which was a lot of money in 1774. His health and mental well-being were soon affected. He suffered from a nervous fever and kidney infection and the 'Dr James Fever Powder' he took probably made things worse. As he lay on his death bed, he was asked if his mind was at ease. His reply and probable last words were, 'No, it is not.'

He is best remembered for his poetry, 'The Deserted Village' and 'The Traveller' being the two works most associated with him, as well as the novel *The Vicar of Wakefield*. After his death, David Garrick, another member of The Club, to which they all belonged, described Goldsmith as follows: 'Here lies Nolly Goldsmith, for shortness called Noll, who wrote like an angel, but talked like poor Poll.'

Goldsmith was buried in the Church of St Mary, London. The Club placed a cenotaph to his honour at Poet's Corner in

Westminster Abbey, London. The epitaph written by his friend Samuel Johnson reads:

> A Poet, Naturalist, and Historian,
> Who left scarcely any style of writing untouched,
> And touched nothing that he did not adorn;
> Of all the passions,
> Whether smiles were moved to tears,
> A powerful yet gentle master;
> In genius, sublime, vivid, versatile,
> In style, elevated, clear, elegant –
> The love of companions,
> The fidelity of friends,
> And the veneration of readers.
> Have by this monument honoured the memory.

Perhaps Goldsmith should have the last word. He once said, 'Our greatest glory consists not in never failing, but in rising every time we fall.'

REFERENCES

'The Literature Network', www.online-literature/ oliver-goldsmith

'Ardagh Village Landscapes', www.ardaghvillagelandscapes.com

'Library Ireland'.

'Dr Oliver Goldsmith', J.H. Plumb, www.ourcivilisation.com

Ardagh Heritage Centre, Annette Corkery, Ardagh, Co. Longford.

Journal of Ardagh and Clonmacnoise Antiquarian Society, Vol. 1, No. 2, pp.92–93.

11

BUTTER STEALING

Butter was one of the few items produced on the farm that could be sold for cash. This part of the family cash flow was essential to the survival of the 'enterprise'. It was usually the butter of no more than three or four cows that was involved. Butter making can be a fickle craft. There are many factors that can influence the almost magical transformation of the liquid milk into the beautiful solid yellow butter. If it failed for the occasional day this was not a problem but if it continued, financial ruin faced a family. Collector Jim Delaney came upon many stories of butter taking, all with very similar elements. Here are stories from Mrs Mary Morris (nee Brady) a 'housewife' from Carrigmaguirk, William Caddow (64), of Rosinurlan, Longford and Francis Clarke (82) from Barragh More, near Drumlish.

Stealing butter, or stealing the profit from the butter, is a common thread through the folk tales of many Irish counties. Longford is no different. In fact, fear of butter stealing is common in other countries' folklore as well. For example, in Stodov, Scandinavia, it was said that there once was a woman who practised witchcraft. When she was making butter, she would say, 'A spoonful of cream from everyone in the county.' From this she always had a churn full of cream for her own butter making.

May Day (1 May) and May Eve were an especially dangerous time for the butter to be 'taken' from the milk. In many places milch cows and calves were kept in an enclosed paddock and watched on the night of May Eve lest anyone, in any form human or otherwise, were to take three teatfuls of milk. If they did, they had your butter for the next twelve months. Hares were particularly suspect. A farmer seeing a hare near his cattle on May Eve would try his best to kill it, believing it to be a witch in disguise determined to drink from the teats of the cows and in doing so rob the profit of the butter.

It was a custom on May Day to never give away any milk, even by way of charity, or to lend any item connected with butter making, e.g. a churn or the dash or any other butter making accessory.

On May Day, farmers would try to have their milking and churning completed before sunrise. This would mean a very early start to the milking that day. Prayers were also said as this day and the ritual of butter making were vital to the economic well-being of the family.

> Bless the cow that gives the milk,
> Bless the milk that gives the cream,
> Bless the cream that gives us the butter,
> Bless us O Lord, Amen.

Mrs Mary Morris (nee Brady) a 'housewife' from Carrigmaguirk, Columcille, gave this story of butter taking. She had heard it from her father, a man born in 1830 and living in the townland of Gelshia, where Mrs Morris had also been reared.

Dan Brady, an uncle of her father, was a farmer. His butter had been gone a long time so this May Morning he got up very early to see what was going on. He was watching from the door of an outhouse where he could see without being seen. He saw this old woman picking 'kippings' or 'buachailláns'. She went up and down the field and kept on collecting until she had filled her apron. 'Bedad! I'll wait no longer,' said Dan to himself. He called a pair of dogs that he had with him and set them after the old woman. She took to her heels and the two dogs after her. One of the dogs chased her to a clump of bushes and cornered her there. She immediately turned into a hare and ran off through the bushes.

Dan went to where she had dropped the buchailláns, picked them up and brought them home. As he had cream ready, he began to churn. Soon he couldn't work the dash as the churn was so stiff with butter.

Many of his neighbours were missing butter at the same time. Dan went to the farms of all these neighbours and gave them some of the buchailláns and they all got their butter back.

Mrs Morris also recalled a story about the McVeighs who lived near Ballinalee.

The McVeighs were losing their butter one time and someone told them that they would get it back if before churning they closed up every nook and cranny in the house, including even the chinks in the doorways. After this an iron would be heated in the fire. The heating of the iron would draw the culprit who was stealing the milk to the house.

One young man who was helping them in the task was so overcome by the heat in the house with everything closed and a roaring fire heating the irons that he fainted and in falling burned his heels quite severely on the irons.

William Caddow (64) told a similar story.

There was a woman living near Rosinurlan, not far from Longford town. She had four cows who gave her milk from which she and her husband churned and made their own butter. They would churn and put the butter in a tub and every week they would add the week's churning to the tub until it was full. When full it held about seventy pounds of butter. They would then take the tub to the butter market in Longford town.

One evening both husband and wife began churning the day's milk. They churned and churned away, but nothing happened. They could get no butter. The man became vexed and claimed that the wife hadn't cleaned the crock properly. They next day they churned again, and nothing happened. This went on for three weeks.

There was a very old man in the area who 'had the cure for witchcraft'. The only time you could visit him was after midnight. The husband went to him one night to get back the butter. He told the old man what was happening and was informed in reply that he already knew all about his situation and that 'someone was takin' his butter'.

The farmer was instructed to go home and told what to do. He was told that when ready to churn again he was to bolt every door, put blinds on the windows and to 'stop up every hole and corner in the house'. He was further told to 'put down a good fire and to put the coulter of the plough into the fire' (the 'coulter' is the knife-like part of a plough). The instructions continued, 'It will begin to get red after a while, when it's getting red begin to churn and let no one into the house.'

The next day the husband and wife did as the old man had instructed. When the coulter began to get red the husband began to churn. He was churning for some time when a loud knocking began at the door. It was an old woman trying to get in. 'Let me in,' she demanded, but they took no notice of her. The old woman began to scream and to kick the door but, although terrified, they ignored her. Eventually she stopped. Somehow the coulter of the plough was burning the old hag outside. At this point the butter was becoming thick. 'It's getting terrible heavy,' said the husband as he worked the dash of the churn. It got so heavy that it was the thickest and best butter they ever had.

The old woman was never seen again, and they never had any trouble with their butter after that.

Francis Clarke (82) from Barragh More, near Drumlish, told this story:

There was a woman who had three cows. Like the previous couple, one time she was churning and churning her milk for hours without it thickening in the slightest. She went to the local priest and asked his help. He told her to go on May Morning to a certain bridge over the river. She went to the bridge as she had been told and waited. She waited for what seemed an eternity but in fact was probably no more than half an hour. She saw an old woman approach the bridge. The old woman was calling, 'Who will rowl [roll] me ball of yarn?' The woman who was losing her butter shouted back, 'I'll rowl yer ball of yarn!' She shouted it three times. When the old woman saw her, she quickly ran away.

The woman losing her butter returned home and never told anyone in the family of her visit to the priest nor the events that had taken place at the bridge. After a while she began to churn as normal and there was so much butter in the churn that they weren't able to lift the dash and 'they had the butter of the country'. If she hadn't been at the bridge to answer the old woman, then the woman who had shouted, 'Who'll rowl me ball of yarn?' would they have got all their butter back?

REFERENCES

https://steelthistles.blogspot.com/2012/12/folklore-snippits-stealing-cream.html

National Museum of Ireland, https://www.museum.ie/Country-Life/Featured-Topics/May-Day/Butter

Killererin Heritage Group, https://killererin.galwaycommunityheritage.org/content/new-contribution

NFC 1429, 55–56, William Caddow (64), Rosinurlan, Longford, Co. Longford. Collector: Jim Delaney.

NFC 1457, 582–583, Francis Clarke (82), Barragh More, Drumlish, Co. Longford. Collector: Jim Delaney.

NFC 1399, 541–542, Mrs Mary Morris (Nee Brady), Carrigmaguirk, Columcille, Co. Longford.

12

THE SLEEPING BEAUTY OF THE LAKE AND OTHER TALES OF LOUGH GOWNA

On the Longford/Cavan border, Lough Gowna provided the setting for some strange happenings in the 1890s. The material for 'The Sleeping Beauty' came from Sean O Suilleabhain in 1992.

Of all the legends and folk tales relating to Lough Gowna, the best-known concerns the case of the 'Sleeping Beauty of Lough Gowna'. There was a young woman who fell into a deep trance and could not be woken. Depending on the version of the story being told, the girl slept for a period ranging from a few months to twenty-two years. Whatever the actual duration, the fact is the girl took no food and very little water for the entire duration of her slumber.

Mary Kate Kavanagh lived with her widowed mother and family in what was described at the time as a miserable little semi-mud-walled cabin. It was located on the Aughnacliffe side of Dernaferst Bridge. The family were poor despite owning a few acres of land. The year was 1893 and Mary Kate was twenty-two years of age.

Mary Kate's 'illness' began in the last few days of 1892. In the period leading up to 1 January, she had suffered from a series of fits and had become delusional. Her mother was very worried about her deteriorating condition and sent for the parish priest of Gowna, Fr Corcoran. Fr Corcoran came and administered the last rites to the girl. The priest had only left the Kavanaghs' cabin a short while when Mary Kate stiffened into a trance, or what was later described by doctors as a 'cataleptic trance'. A 'cataleptic trance' is a very rare but recognised medical condition. It is deemed to be as much a psychiatric problem as a physical condition and is often associated with people of a highly nervous or hysterical nature. The condition includes a rigidity of the body and a complete insensibility. Typically, the condition is of short duration and last only minutes or days at most. It was in this state that Mary Kate remained. She was rigid, motionless and unresponsive even to having pins stuck into her body. What is unique about her case is the length of time the trance lasted.

The story of the girl in suspended animation quickly spread not just throughout the local district but also through the county. Many people said she had become a changeling and had been 'taken by the fairies'. When the case first came to his attention, Dr Winslow, the local dispensary doctor for the Gowna area, came and examined Mary on 16 January. Dr Winslow diagnosed the girl to be in a cataleptic trance. While her pulse and temperature were normal, there was much about her condition that was not. The doctor reported that if any of her limbs were raised, they would remain in that position for any length of time until they were repositioned again.

Her mouth was tightly clenched, and it was only with great difficulty that the doctor managed to open it slightly, so some liquids could be given to her. The doctor noted that even then most of the liquid just ran from the corners of her mouth. No solid food passed her lips. Fearing that the girl would die from malnutrition or dehydration, he decided to use 'faradisation'. Faradisation involved the application of electric shocks to the patient from a battery, what would today be described as ECT treatment. Dr Winslow, with the help of Dr Kenny from Granard, administered the treatment. Mary Kate gave no reaction whatsoever when the electric current was applied. This was something the good doctors thought to be very strange.

Doctors Winslow and Kenny had no doubt about the genuine-ness of Mary Kate's condition, however baffling it appeared. Word of the girl's condition spread through the medical world following the publication of an article on the case by Dr Winslow in the *British Medical Journal*. On 9 May 1893 four doctors visited the girl: Dr Winslow and Dr Kenny, who were already very famil-iar with the case, and Dr Yorke and Dr Cochrane, both from Longford town. Dr Cochrane, who had a very strong personality, took the lead role in the examination of the young girl. He used very drastic measures to awaken her, sticking needles into her and pulling her from her bed and dragging her around the room very violently. This drastic treatment failed to wake her from her trance. It was also stated that Dr Cochrane used a stomach pump and chloroform (one would imagine that chloroform would have the opposite effect to waking the girl).

Dr Cochrane claimed that when the doctors entered her room the girl had her eyes open but when they reached her bed her eyes were closed. No effort on the part of Dr Cochrane managed to get them open.

After the examination, Dr Cochrane was convinced the girl was an imposter faking her condition. This, along with the doc-tor's violent treatment of Mary Kate, was the start of a major controversy. Some claimed he was right, and his examination had been very professionally carried out, while others felt the girl's condition was genuine and that the good doctor's behav-iour had been anything but professional.

The parish priest, Fr Corcoran, was outraged by the treat-ment of the girl and the claims that it was all a hoax. He wrote to the *Roscommon Herald* on 10 June 1893 and put his views on record. The four doctors remained split in their opinions: Doctors Winslow and Kenny maintained the genuineness of the case, while doctors Cochrane and Yorke defended the examination and Dr Cochrane's conclusions. Fr Corcoran threw down the gauntlet to Dr Yorke. He demanded that two medical men and one layman carry out a fresh and thorough re-examination of Mary Kate. He said he was willing to donate £20 to a charity of Dr Yorke's choosing 'if it can be shown that there was a particle of deceit, fraud or imposture in this case from the beginning'. The challenge was conditional on the other doctors making a similar donation.

Naturally the case created great interest, not just among the medical practitioners but among the people of the locality. There was a constant flow of people wanting to see Mary Kate. All this attention upset Mrs Kavanagh and she became very unwelcoming of sightseers. Local opinion was divided between those who believed that Mary Kate was an imposter and those who believed she had been 'taken by the fairies'. Some people went to great lengths to gain access to the girl's bedroom. Two young men later identified as the brothers Gerard and Patrick Byrne ended up in court for their attempts. They had arrived at the cottage during the afternoon of 3 June while Mrs Kavanagh was away. They somehow gained access and used burning matches to awaken the girl. When Mrs Kavanagh returned, she found the door of the cottage wide open and Mary Kate lying on the floor. The bedclothes had been thrown in a corner and the sash window had been removed. There was a smell of burnt matches and some had been thrown on the floor. It was suspected that Dr Cochrane was behind these further 'tests' but it was never proven. The young men admitted being in the cottage but were acquitted of all charges.

By June, Dr Winslow, who was Mary Kate's main doctor, reported that her limbs were not as rigid as they had been earlier in the year and when spoken to she was able to look at the speaker. It is generally believed that Mary Kate did eventually recover.

What happened to the Kavanaghs? The mother and daughter left the area sometime after 1901 but there is uncertainty what happened after that. Some said they went to England, others that they had moved north. The general belief locally is that Mary Kate eventually married. One thing remains certain and that is that the legend of 'The Sleeping Beauty of Gowna' lives on.

How did Lough Gowna get its name? One story of its formation was given in the 1930s by a Mrs Connolly (75) who lived in Ballinalee.

Lough Gowna means 'the lake of the calf'. 'Gamhain' is a calf born in November, which used to be known as 'Gam'. The name 'Gam' comes from a Greek word for wedding, because in olden times many people married in November. 'Gamnach' is also the Irish for a milch cow with a year-old calf.

According to legend, Lough Gowna wasn't always there as it is today. Many, many years ago in the time of St Colmcille, the saint was travelling in the area. In what is now the parish of Colmcille, in the townland of Dring, there was a holy well used by all the local people. The well had been specially blessed by the saint for their special use. Because of its veneration, it was treated as a very sacred place, one that was treated with great respect.

Great respect by everyone that is except a certain lady who came to the well one day. This lady brought all her dirty clothes, dresses, undergarments, bedclothes and proceeded to wash them in the waters that had been blessed by St Colmcille.

As the woman washed her clothes and the dirt from them spread through the well, a wild sort of calf jumped up through the ground. The old woman got the fright of her life. She watched as the calf stampeded from Dring to Arvagh. This is a distance of six or seven miles. What really struck terror into the woman was that the water of the well followed the calf all the way. The calf's gallop was finally stopped by a farmer who was mowing his land in the path of the oncoming calf and water. He swung his scythe, cutting the legs from the calf, and that was where the water stopped. The result was the forming of Lough Gowna. Sadly, the well dried up, much to the disappointment of the people locally not to mention the remorse of the woman who had desecrated the well.

Near Aughnacliff, off the shore of Lough Gowna, is the island of Inchmore. The island has long been associated with St Colmcille. It was said that St Colmcille founded the original monastery on the island. In the twelfth century, the monks on the island, who lived a very hard life, adopted the rule of St Augustine and this continued until all the monasteries in the country were dissolved by Henry VIII in 1543, bringing to an end the monastic life that had been part of the island for almost one thousand years. Today the ruins of the monastery and a graveyard are all that remain.

In the 1930s Pat Rogers (53), of Ballinalee, Co. Longford, had an interesting tale about the island. Pat said he had heard this story from his mother.

Long, long ago, a lone stranger was seen walking along the shores of Lough Gowna. He would stop every now and again to look at the beautiful island out in the lake. He eventually retraced his steps and walked to a farmer's house nearby. He walked in the door with a 'God save all here'. The farmer replied with a courteous 'God save you kindly'.

The stranger then asked the farmer if he could borrow the huge flag that was in front of the fireside. The farmer told him he could borrow it with pleasure but that it would take twenty men to lift it. To the farmer's amazement, the stranger stretched his arms across the whole width of the flag, touched it with his fingers and lifted the great flag as if it were only a sheet of paper.

The stranger then carried the flag to the lake shore, watched by the shocked farmer and his family. He placed the flagstone on the water, where it floated just like a boat. The mystery man then stepped on the flag and floated off across the lake to the island of Inchmore. After being on the island for only a short time, the stranger floated back on the flagstone to the lake shore. All the while the farmer and his entire family watched proceedings in awe.

The stranger went up to the farmer and thanked him for his kindness. When the farmer and his family went back into their cottage, they were again amazed. Where the flagstone originally lay, they saw the most beautiful fireplace that seemed to them to have appeared from nowhere. It was later revealed that the mysterious stranger was none other than St Colmcille himself.

From that day on and for more than one hundred years the people of the area were able to float from the shore to the island. A church and graveyard were established, and the floating flag was also used to transport corpses to the graveyard on the island during their funerals.

A sudden end came to the floating flagstone when one day a group of merrymakers were using the stone to get to the island. According to Pat Roger's mother, the merrymakers must have been sinners. The flag broke in two and sank to the bottom while in the middle of the lake. All those on the stone at the time were drowned. The flagstone was never seen again.

REFERENCES

NFCS 0766, 61, Mrs Connolly (75), Ballinalee, Co. Longford.
    Clonbroney, Meathus Truim, 1938, Ss Ó Conchobhair.
www.irishidentity.com/extras/island/stories/provinces.htm
https://archive.org/stream/placenamesofcou00macg/place-
    namesofcou00macg_djvu.txt
Teathbha, Vol. 2, No. 3, 1992.

13

The Gate House on the Fairy Mound

Dr Bob Curran is a native of Co. Down but currently lives near The Giant's Causeway, Co. Antrim, with his family. He is a prolific author with more than thirty books to his credit. One of his areas of specialisation is the supernatural and otherworldly matters. The incident below happened while Bob was working on his book Irish Tales from the Otherworld *and relates to an incident he experienced while travelling through Co. Longford.*

There are hundreds of fairy mounds, raths, paths and generally places regarded as having a 'presence'. This presence is what was described in classical Roman beliefs as a *genius loci* or 'protective spirit' of a place. There have been many tales of people building on such locations with disastrous consequences. These can include problems with the structure of the actual building, strange happenings or more simply a malign feeling associated with the building.

While travelling through Longford some years ago, Bob Curran was told there was just such a 'sheehogue' somewhere between Granard and Edgeworthstown. At the time he was researching the Forbes family, the Earls of Granard. During his research he was told to contact a certain old couple who it was thought knew something of the ruins of a house once owned by the Forbes.

He found the couple's cottage and was welcomed in true Longford tradition. Curran began asking about the ruins and what if anything the couple knew of the house and whoever had lived there. The man of the house had worked the land and farmed around the ruins for many years. He said the house was originally owned by the Forbes family but for many years the lands had been owned by a series of local landowners. In fact, the man seemed to know very little about the house that had once stood there.

He said, 'The old house might have been haunted … but it was the gate house that was dangerous.' The farmer told Bob that he had been told by his grandfather that the gate house to the estate had been built on a fairy mound. Even in his grandfather's time the gate house remained unoccupied, but it had always been considered a 'bad place'. The farmer added the opinion that there were 'things that live in them places that never go away … People sometimes mistake them for ghosts and fairies, but they're not – they might be far older, for they were here when men first came to Ireland.'

The Forbes were advised not to dig up the mound nor to build their gate house here, but they did. The result was that from the time it was completed, the gate house had a very ominous presence about it. Every family who had tried to live in it had left very soon after moving in, such was the nature of the *genius loci* there.

Some years earlier a retired clergyman from Northern Ireland had moved into the gate house. The house had been purchased by friends of the clergyman and he was renting it from them. He was in the process of writing a book and wanted a quiet retreat. He only stayed in the cottage a short while. A series of strange sounds, things being moved mysteriously about the cottage and a heavy feeling as if someone or something was continually watching, drove the good clergyman away.

On one occasion while the clergyman was still in the house the farmer was down doing some odd jobs for him. The reverend asked him, 'John, are you a good whistler?' John, the farmer, thought it was a strange question because he was

unable to whistle a note. Any time he tried he just blew air. To this the clergyman said, 'If it's not you, who is it? I sometimes hear some-body whistling round the back of the house. A very strong whistle, but tuneless – no melody to it.' There was never anybody else around the house, or that's as it seemed. However, there was always a heaviness in the air, a sense that someone was behind you but if you turned quickly there was never anybody visible.

On another occasion the reverend called on John to check the drains because the most terrible smell had begun to invade the cottage. John thoroughly checked all the drains and although he found nothing, he too got 'a heavy, rotten, sickening stench, like something that had died'. No matter how hard he tried, John could find nothing. The strangest thing about this smell was that on some occasions it was present and on others there was not a trace of it.

It was the smell that finally drove the clergyman away from the cottage as he found it impossible to live, work and write in that environment.

Curran asked John if he or his wife had ever seen anything strange around the cottage. The farmer said he hadn't but had often experienced the smells and whistling. He added that some people say it's ghosts about the place, but he described it as the 'Thing'. He then asked Dr Curran if he would he like to visit the gate house as he had the key.

On the walk from the farmer's cottage towards the gate house John confided to Curran that while he had said that he hadn't seen anything, that was untrue. His wife was of a 'nervous disposition' and he hadn't wanted to frighten her. He had on more than one occasion seen something. One evening he was on his way to the gate house, where he often went for a conversation, a pipe and a glass of whiskey with the clergyman. He clearly saw the shape of a man walk to the end of the garden. John said it was a 'low-set man with a hat of some sort and dressed in a very old-fashioned way. The "Thing" turned and walked back towards the gate house, and as it did it began to fade away like smoke and then there was nothing there. It walked in a funny, almost jumping way that didn't look like a human walk at all.' When he was with the reverend, he didn't say anything of what he had seen but the clergyman said that he had heard the whistling again that evening just before John had arrived. John said that he had seen strange things on different occasions but was reluctant to speak about them.

At this stage Bob and John had turned a corner in the lane and in front of them stood the gate house and beside it the remains of two pillars, all that was left of the gate posts of the old driveway. It was much smaller than Dr Curran had imagined. It was architecturally like many gate houses that are seen at the gates to big estates but this one was different in other ways. While it was a very mild evening there was a 'coldness' and a 'distinct air of menace' emanating from the building. The old farmer suddenly stopped. 'There it is,' said he, 'but this is as far as I'll go. Go ahead if you want a closer look but I'll not go. I'll wait for you here.' He said this with a definite unease. He clearly didn't want to be anywhere near the building.

Not sure that he really wanted to proceed, Bob took the key, approached the overgrown front door and with difficulty managed to get it open. He was struck by a scene of total dereliction and abandonment. Over and above the obvious mustiness of an old unlived-in building was a feeling of 'oppression' and 'watchfulness'. The building was small, and it didn't take long to examine the rooms until he was at the back of the house. He turned to walk back to the front door. As he did so he felt something invisible physically push against him in an effort to get past or even do him harm. While it only lasted seconds, the sensation was very unsettling. There had definitely been something there and it had felt as if the whole house was alive with it.

Curran was very glad to make the front door and 'escape' into the daylight beyond. When he reached him, he told the old farmer of what he had experienced. John just nodded and said he wouldn't enter that building even he was offered a fortune to do so.

In the days following his experience, Dr Curran rationalise what he had experienced but he could not. Perhaps the old farmer had been right and the gate house had been built on some ancient prehistoric mounds, a sacred place that had been violated and forces unleashed that were better not disturbed.

Some years later Dr Curran was back in the same area but was unable to find where the gate house had been. He could find no trace of it. Even the house where the old couple had lived was gone. Where he thought he remembered it to have been there was a high builder's fence and the whole site was marked for development. If building work has gone on there since Curran's initial visit, has the 'Thing' moved on or is it still there waiting for the next people to come along? I hope not.

REFERENCE

Irish Tales from the Otherworld, pp.293–308, Dr Bob Curran, Poolbeg Press, 2008.

14

STOLEN CHILDREN

The following stories were told by Bernard Reilly (82) of Cullinmore, Granard, Co. Longford, to folklore collector Philip Ledwith.

Around the year 1820 there lived a woman and her husband in the townland of Drumhalry who had only one child. It was a girl of tender years still in her infancy. She was always kept in the cradle right under the kitchen window where she could be under the constant vigilance of her mother. She was a beautiful child and very quiet. She was never known to cry, no matter what happened. The parents really doted on her.

This happy state continued until she was about three years of age. An immediate neighbour, no relation to the parents of the child, was working close by at harvesting operations. As he worked, he saw two hooded women going in the direction of the child's home. They came from a section of the field where no gap or recognised path existed. They went straight up to the window under which the child was sleeping.

The farmer harvesting kept a very close eye on their movements. From the first moment he had seen them he suspected that there was some sort of witchery afoot. They took some implements from under their cloaks and commenced unfastening the window. The harvester pretended not to see them, and the two women worked on the window until the underneath half had been unfastened and taken away.

One of the women stretched her arms through the aperture, lifted the child from the cradle and gathered her in under her cloak. The other woman then stepped over to the window and took from under her cloak a bundle that looked like another child. She pushed the bundle through the window and let it drop into the cradle where the baby had been sleeping.

They then took to their heels, crossing a fence with great agility. They had gone some distance before the farmer harvesting was able to react. The farmer, with the help of his sheepdog, pursued them and managed to head them off. He demanded that they surrender the child. The two women protested violently that they were not in possession of any child but after a number of threats they handed the child to him.

He took the baby girl back to his house, gave her some milk and put her in the bed to rest after the terrifying experience. The child started to cry. It was the first time the child was heard crying by anyone. She soon settled down, seemingly unaware that she was in the house of a neighbour. The farmer did not tell the parents of the stolen child that he had rescued her until much later.

Meanwhile, the parents of the baby girl discovered that something was wrong and that the child in their cradle did not in any way resemble their own child. They became frantic with grief and desolation. At the time their child was stolen, they were totally unaware of it. They had been at the other end of the house, some distance away from the kitchen.

When the mother returned to what she believed to be her own child, all she saw was a pale, diminutive, sickly, ugly wicked and dirty baby who screamed and made horrible noises, unlike those of a human child. The child continued to cry for almost a week. This child would hardly eat, drink nor sleep. Nothing could pacify it. It died around the seventh day at the exact hour that it had been exchanged for the genuine child.

During the seven days the parents were distracted and consulted priests and doctors to see if they could do anything about it. They were told by the parish priest to give the child one cup of milk per day, just to keep it from starving. The priest knew as soon as he saw 'it' that it had been placed there by the fairies and would not live for very long.

The parents' grief for their own lost child was very touching. They did not know what else to do and turned to the practice of making charms to see if it would restore their own lost child. All of this was, of course, to no avail.

The farmer who had rescued the stolen baby sat tight and did not disclose the whereabouts of the missing child for about three weeks. His fear was that the fairies would return in force and spirit the child away. There was a belief that after the elapse of twenty-one days the fairies were unable to cast any further spells on a particular baby.

After the three weeks had elapsed, the farmer, accompanied by his ever-faithful sheepdog, took the baby and brought it back to his neighbour, the baby's mother. Great was their joy on receiving their precious child back to its rightful home where she had given the parents so much joy.

The baby grew to be a beautiful young maiden and married a very prosperous merchant. The young couple lived a happy and prosperous ever afterwards. However, not so the farmer who had rescued the young maiden when she was a baby. His cattle died and his own children met with misfortune. He sold out his farm and set sail for America.

The ship encountered many storms on the wild Atlantic. Finally, when they were in sight of America, the ship was hit by a terrible storm, a storm that proved to be one storm too many. The ship floundered and sank, with only a few survivors succeeding in reaching the shore. Unfortunately, the farmer who had rescued the child all those years earlier was not one of them.

The people living in the district around Drumhalry eventually heard of the tragic drowning of their once-while neighbour. It was generally believed that the fairies had finally had their revenge on the man who had deprived them of a human child. Bernard Reilly, who told this story, said he had heard it from his father, who had no doubt whatsoever about its truthfulness. The generation of his father referred to the incident as fact and put it down to one of the things that frequently happened to those who interfere with the fairies.

ANOTHER STOLEN CHILD

This man lived on his farm with his wife and young son, who was aged about four. The father was constantly attending to his duties on the farm and had the habit of taking his son along with him everywhere he went.

They could be seen together early and late driving the cows, taking them home at night to be milked and foddered, visiting distant fields and pastureland to inspect fences. During all these activities the little boy could be seen trotting after his dad. Sometimes the boy would become tired and want to rest. His father would take off his coat, spread it on the ground and let the boy lie on it to rest and perhaps fall asleep. Sometimes the father would himself fall asleep, especially if the day was warm. The father ensured he was in 'quick reach' of the boy at all times.

This idyllic lifestyle continued for some time. In the evenings the father would tell his wife of all the little talks that occurred between himself and their son. They were a very happy family until one evening just before dusk an old hag came to their door and asked for a charity. The little boy, who was also present, went towards the old hag and insisted on standing up beside her, apparently wanting to make friends with her. His mother objected very strongly to him having anything to do with the old woman and made him stand away from her.

The old woman took this as a terrible insult. She commenced to mumble under her breath for some time. She then told the boy's mother to keep him from going about too much with his father, warning that if she didn't, she would be sorry. The hag then withdrew from the house after some further mumblings. The mother went to the door to see the direction in which the old woman had gone. She was surprised and more than a little shocked that she could see neither 'sign nor light' of her anywhere. The mother was immediately seized with a terrible fear and became convinced that the old 'woman' was in fact not a real woman but a forerunner of some misfortune to come.

Time went by and no misfortune struck the family. Before long the incident faded and was soon all but forgotten. The household settled down and quickly returned to their simple but idyllic lifestyle. One day the father took the boy on their usual rounds of tasks all over the farm. After they had inspected one of the furthest pastures from the house the little boy said he was tired. The father, as usual, took off his coat and made the lad lie down on it for a rest. The boy soon fell asleep as the father watched over him. As the father sat surveying his land, he noticed what he thought was a fallen fence pole nearby. He wandered over to straighten the stake.

His was away from the boy for no more than ten minutes but when he returned to where the boy was sleeping, he found his son to be dead. Beside the lifeless body were two objects, one a tiny little red peaked cap made from rushes. It had three tassels attached, one in front, one at the back and one on top of the crown. The other object was a piece of parchment-like paper with an indecipherable scrawl written on it.

The grief of the parents was unbearable as they buried the

lifeless body of their precious son. For long after the son's death the father showed the cap and the parchment to anyone he thought might be able to offer an explanation as to their significance. No such insights were ever forthcoming. The only opinion that seemed to fit was that the cap and the paper were some sort of warning against treating the old hag with contempt as she meekly asked for alms.

Eventually they were placed in a cupboard. The father and mother would often go to the cupboard and hold the two items, a last connection with their dead son. On one final occasion as it turned out, the mother went to the press only to discover that they had gone missing, never to be seen again.

Hughie Corrigan and the Girl that was Taken

This is one of the stories of Francis Clarke (82) of Barragh More. What is particularly interesting in this story is that it was told by Francis in the house where some of the events took place. The story here is written as closely as possible to the way Jim Delaney (JD) faithfully reproduced everything said by Mr Clarke.

There was a fair used to be here in Drumlish at Hollandtide (November Eve, Halloween) and they used to be all hurryin' up to get out the spuds to have a day's comfort at the fair. They was all risin' early and workin' to have them out.

There was two boys, Corrigan's, livin in this house with their mother [by the time of this telling the house was Mr Clarke's home]. They were up early this mornin' and they went out. There was a heavy frost on the ground and down by the river on the other side they saw a woman and her lyin' with her head towards a bit of risin' ground. The two stood on the riverbank and was afraid to cross over the river because they thought she was dead, and it is unlucky to find a dead man or a woman.

They went across at last anyhow and the woman was breathin' but wasn't conscious. They stirred her up anyway and the first thing she said was, 'Where am I?' and they told her she was in Barragh More.

So, they brought her up to the house. Their mother was up in that room [here Frank Clarke pointed to a bedroom off the kitchen JD] in bed and after givin' her a sup o' tay they brought the young woman up to the mother. 'We have a present for you Mother,' says they.

'What is it Jewel?' says the auld woman.

So, she put on her clothes and got up to attend to the young woman. They got from her that she was from the parish of Mohill.

Anyway, she stopped here till the Fair of Drumlish at Hollandtide. One of the men from this house (Corrigan's) was at the fair and he met this man from the parish of Mohill. 'Matt,' he says to him, 'how are you getting' on?'

'Well not so good Hughie,' he says, 'I lost the finest girl in the parish of Mohill. Ten days ago, we buried her.'

'How long did you say?' says Corrigan.

'Ten days ago,' says the man, and the man was very lonesome for his daughter.

The Fair of Arva was comin' on the next day and the Mohill man bought nothin' in Drumlish Fair but said he would go to the Arva Fair the next day. Hughie Corrigan says to him, 'Come down with us,' he says, 'There's no use in your goin' home tonight and you goin' to Arva Fair tomorrow.'

So, he went home with Corrigan that evenin' and when he saw the girl in Corrigan's he fainted. It was his daughter that he thought he had buried ten days ago. She was taken by the fairies. He brought her home with him and sent her to America and Pat Corrigan that took her from the ground that October mornin' be the river met her afterwards in America and married her.

REFERENCES

NFC 1021 OR 1022: 7–13, Bernard Reilly (87), Granard, Co. Longford. Collector: Philip Ledwith, March 1947.

NFC 1457, 613–615, Frank Clarke (82), Farmer, Barragh More, Drumlish, Co. Longford. Jim Delaney.

15

The Pot of Gold

This story is based on a story collected in 1936 by Patrick MacCabe (14) who was a pupil at Lislea School, Ballinalee. Patrick had heard it from his mother, who in turn had heard it from her father, 'Grey' Pat Gill of Edenmore, Ballinamuck. 'Grey' Pat had heard it from his own father. This story is very similar to a well-known English folk tale called 'The Pedlar of Swaffham'. Swaffham is a small town in Norfolk and there is a monument in the town to the pedlar, John Chapman. There are similar legends throughout Europe and the Middle East. The earliest known version dates from a thirteenth-century Persian poet.

Once upon a time a man and his wife lived at the back of Corn Hill, between Drumlish and Ballinalee, in the parish of Killoe. They were farmers but struggled to survive each year, always worrying that something small but unexpected would come and tip them from survival into destitution. They never experienced a year when they had plenty and were able to relax. Theirs was a constant struggle. They had a small one-roomed low cottage with a lone bush at its gable end. The cottage and bush were surrounded by an old wall with a gate painted red leading into the cottage.

One night the man had a dream, a very vivid dream. In the dream he dreamed that if he went to the Bridge of London, he would find a pot of gold. Despite the clarity and vividness of the dream, the farmer knew it was nonsense. Here he was living in the middle of Ireland. He had seldom even crossed the borders of Co. Longford, let alone make a journey to the city of London in England. Nothing but pipe dreams.

Night after night he had the same dream. The same in every detail. He said nothing to his wife as he knew she would only call him an 'amadán' (fool). The dreams continued, never changing in detail, never changing in their message: go to the Bridge of London and you will find a pot of gold.

Eventually, he felt he would burst if he didn't tell his wife. One day as they ate their simple dinner of potatoes and buttermilk, he told his wife about the dream and about it repeating every night. Her reaction was as he feared. 'Arrah, stop your raving,' she said. 'To go on such a long journey with all the associated expense and for what?' She added for emphasis, 'For nothing, that's what.'

Despite her objections, he decided he was going to go anyway such was the pull the dream had on him by this stage. That night, the night he made the decision to go to London and all the associated risks, he once again had the same dream.

While it was the same dream, there was more in the dream this time. In that night's dream, he dreamed that at the Bridge of London he would meet a man on the bridge who would tell him exactly where he would find his pot of gold. The following day he set out on his journey, the journey of a lifetime. This journey would either make him and his wife comfortable for life or condemn him as the world's biggest fool. As he left their little cottage it wasn't words of encouragement from his wife that rang in his ears but words that highlighted all his fears about the journey on which he was embarking.

He walked to Edgeworthtown and got the train to Dublin. He had never been in Dublin, never mind London. He was terrified. The crowds, the hustle and bustle all made him want to turn around and get back with his tail between his legs to Corn Hill. He didn't flinch, instead he purchased a return ferry and train ticket from Dublin to London. After buying his ticket, he was almost penniless. This only added to his sense of insecurity and fear. The journey from Dublin to London was uneventful but he was tense and frightened every step of the way.

When the boat train arrived at London's Paddington Station, he asked directions to the Bridge of London. After many detours and often getting lost, he finally saw before his eyes the Bridge of London.

It was a busy, busy place. People crossed the bridge both ways as they went about their business. As he was walking across the bridge, he saw a man walking on the other side. This man looked familiar. He looked like someone that had been in the Longford man's dreams. With great difficulty he crossed the bridge and approached the stranger.

'Is it any harm to ask you why you are walking here?' he asked the Londoner.

'Not one bit,' answered the Londoner. The English man said, 'For nights now I've been having this dream. In the dream I keep meeting a man who is looking for a pot of gold. I can never make out his features, but I know he is not from these parts. The strangest thing is that this man doesn't know where the pot of gold lies despite the fact that it is almost under his feet. He lives with his wife in a small one-roomed low cottage with a lone bush at its gable end. The cottage and bush are surrounded by an old wall with a gate painted red leading into the cottage. There is a pot of gold lying underneath the lone bush.'

The man from Corn Hill let out a gasp and exclaimed, 'That's my house and my travels have not been in vain.'

Both men stood on the middle of the bridge dumbstruck as the hustle and bustle of London passed by. When they both had gathered their senses, the Irish man said to his new-found English friend, 'Will you come back to Ireland with me and if you are accurate in what you have just told me I'll give you half the gold as a reward?' He added, 'That would seem to be the fair and honourable thing to do.'

'I will,' said the Londoner, 'I'll return with you this very minute.'

They retraced the journey that the Longford man had taken. There was a great sense of excitement between the pair at the prospect of the riches they hoped to find. Eventually, they stood outside the little cottage just behind Corn Hill. The Londoner exclaimed, 'That's the cottage I saw in my dreams!'

The Longford man's wife was at the door to greet them. The two men spent very little time in pleasantries but quickly got to work with 'loy' and fork and began to dig underneath the bush. They hadn't been digging for more than about ten minutes when the 'loy' struck something solid. They cleared away some more soil and there was a large flagstone. When they had cleared the flag, they lifted it and underneath was a large pot of gold. The two men were ecstatic.

They jumped, danced, shouted at their good fortune. While they were busy in their celebrations, the farmer's wife noticed that there was an inscription on the flag. She cleaned away the remaining soil with her apron and there cut into the flag was, 'One side of the pot is as good as the other.' She shouted at the men to stop gallivanting and to come look. They did. They read the inscription and began to dig on the other side to where the flag had lain. Sure enough, they found another large pot of gold, equal in measure to the first pot they had discovered.

When they had the two pots, they went into the cottage and counted their riches. Each pot was of equal value. True to his word, the Longford man gave one pot to the Londoner and kept the other for himself and his wife. The Englishman stayed a few days with the couple and then returned to England.

What happened to all parties after that is not known. But one thing is for sure, they never wanted for anything again for the rest of their lives.

Reference

NFCS 766, 101–102, Mrs MacCabe, Aughagreagh, Colmcille, Co. Longford. Patrick MacCabe (14), Lislea National School, Ballinalee, 1936, Pádraig Mac Gréine.

16

Best Foot Forward

This story is based on one told in 2003 by Patrick Green when he was 103 years old. This is the same Padraig Mac Greaine whose lifetime passion was the collecting of folk tales from every corner of Co. Longford. The stories he collected are held in the National Folklore Collection and fill more than two thousand pages, providing an incredibly rich vein of Ireland's folklore and traditions.

Near the village of Ballinalee on the banks of the River Camlin there lived a farmer named Mick Farrell. Like most country men, Mick could best be described as they say in North Longford as being 'a right card'. He was also cute. From time to time, but not that often, his business would take him into Longford town itself. He was a tall, well-built man who always wore a distinctive 'Bull's Wool' coat similar in material to that used by the Irish Army for their old uniform great coats. He was also known for the heavy boots he used wear.

One day he was on the road making his purposeful way to Longford when he met his old friend Paddy from Killoe heading in the same direction. It is well known that two shorten the road, so they fell into easy conversation as they travelled.

On arrival into Longford, Mick made straight for a long-established emporium that sold gents' clothes and shoes. The two boys headed into the shop and were greeted by the assistant, who enquired if he could be of assistance. Not one to beat around the bush, Mick demanded in his booming voice to know if the shop sold clogs. The sales assistant answered a little intimidated that they did and that the price was three shillings a pair. Mick said be that as it may but that he only wanted one clog, a right one to be exact because he already had a left one at home.

'Oh,' said the shopkeeper, 'I couldn't do that as we only sell them in pairs.'

Mick then told him his predicament. Not but a few weeks earlier he had attended a fair to sell a cow. He sold the cow and got a better than fair price for her. Naturally such a good deal required a bit of celebration and he had headed to the nearest pub for a 'few' pints. After the few pints, the excitement of the deal and the general exertions of the day, he was more than a little tired by the time he got home. He had dozed off beside the fire but must have been a bit too close to it as the right clog had gone on fire! Apart from costing him an almost new clog, he had almost lost a leg into the bargain. That was why he now only needed one clog, a right clog.

The sales assistant restated the position that the clogs were only sold in pairs, adding with a little temerity that Mick already knew that. 'So, can't you buy yourself a new pair?'

'What in the name of God and the dead generations would I be doing with three clogs when I only have two legs?' demanded Mick. All this time Paddy was watching on in silent amazement.

This was all beginning to tell on the sales assistant and in desperation he said, 'Look, on account of who it is, I'll sell you a pair for two and six pence. That's giving you a special discount of six pence.'

Mick looked at his friend Paddy with a look somewhere between frustration and desperation. Then he looked at the assistant. 'All I want is the right one and two and six is far too dear for a single clog. Look-it, I'll give you one and nine for them.'

'I can't do that,' said the assistant. 'They're three shillings and I'm already letting you have them for two and six.'

'Ah that's still too much.' Getting more and more desperate, the sales assistant said, 'All right, all right I'll let you have them for two shillings.'

'You're a hard man and you drive a hard bargain, but I'll take them off your hands.' The new clogs were duly wrapped up and handed to Mick, who in turn handed over the two shillings.

When they got outside the shop and a good way down the street Paddy, who had become bewildered by Mick's negotiations, asked him what he was trying to do. Mick turned to him, winked and said, 'Sure I never burned a clog so now I have two pairs, and that Paddy is known as putting yer best foot forward!'

REFERENCE

Fireside Tales, Jude Flynn, Longford, 2003.

17

HEMPENSTALL – 'THE WALKING GALLOWS'

Although generally associated with the 1798 Rebellion in Co. Wicklow, 'Hempenstall: The Walking Gallows', carried out his reign of terror not only in that county but also in counties Longford and Westmeath. Many folk stories abound about this brute.

Edward Lambert Hepenstal was born in or about 1776 in Upper Newcastle, Co. Wicklow. When he was a young adult, he trained for and became an apothecary in Dublin. In that role he might have remained in obscurity, but his infamy grew after the restructuring of the militia regiments throughout the country following the establishment of the Society of United Irishmen in 1791. Their aim was to overthrow the Kingdom of Ireland, severing the connection with Great Britain and establishing an Irish Republic based on the principles of the French Revolution. To counter this threat, the Parliament of Ireland reorganised the existing militia in preparation for the risk of invasion by Napoleon and rebellion in Ireland.

Hepenstal (better known as Hempenstall) managed through the influence of his brother, who worked with the Dublin police, to secure a commission with the 37th Wicklow Regiment of Militia. In 1795 he attained the rank of lieutenant. Hepenstal, was, to put it mildly, physically a very noteworthy character. He was described as 'Towering to almost seven feet with chest and muscles in proportion'. The barrister and judge Sir Jonah Barrington wrote in his memoirs (1827), 'I knew him well and from his countenance should never have suspected him of cruelty, but so cold blooded and eccentric an execution of the human race never yet existed.' Barrington summed him up as a 'handsome but brutal giant'.

The mere mention of his name struck terror throughout Wicklow and North Leinster, particularly Westmeath and Longford. The 37th Wicklow Militia were transferred from Wicklow and garrisoned in Mullingar in 1797. It was from here that Hepenstal carried out his reign of terror in Co. Longford.

Lt Hepenstal liked to hang or 'half-hang' his victims by placing a noose around their necks and then, using his great height, lift them from the ground and walk around with them strung by the neck over his back. For this task he usually used the rope from a drum, but failing that used his own silk cravat. Hepenstal was very indiscriminate in the selection of his victims. It was enough for him to dislike a poor wretch for him to dispense summary 'justice' with his methods.

After the Battle of Ballinamuck, a small band of the Co. Longford insurgents under the command of Deniston from Clonbroney, O'Keefe from Prospect and Pat Farrell from Ballinree retreated to Granard.

According to James P. Farrell, 'Above all other places in the county there is none so well adapted, in every sense of the word, to warfare as the town and neighbourhood of Granard. The town is almost surrounded by hills, and on the moat alone a thousand men could keep a hundred thousand in check, such are the facilities for defence.'

At that time Granard was under the control of that 'fearful tyrant' Hepenstal, The Walking

Gallows. Using his great height and method of hanging he had 'jerked more men into eternity' about the neighbourhood of Granard than could be imagined.

When the small band of retreating rebels arrived in Granard from Ballinamuck, they found the whole place in a state of confusion and uproar. People were running about in terror. They were expecting British troops from Ballinalee and more from Cavan to arrive in their town. The sight of three local and well-known leaders even with their small band of rebels steadied the Granard citizens. After brief discussion it was unanimously agreed to make a bold stand for liberty and to defend their town.

The rebels were stationed at the different approaches to the town under the command of Deniston, O'Keefe and O'Farrell. O'Farrell was positioned to defend the approach to the town from Finea. The first of the enemy to appear were the troops from Finea under the command of the hated Hepenstal, who had gone to Cavan to bring these troops into action as fast as possible. O'Farrell was a very tall and well-built man. He stood a full seven feet high with broad chest and great strength. If ever there was a physical match for Hepenstal, it was O'Farrell.

The rebels defending Granard and the attacking militia soon engaged. It was only a short while before O'Farrell and Hepenstal stood face to face. O'Farrell struck Hepenstal a single blow with the hilt of his broken sword and felled the opposing giant. The troops that Hepenstal commanded took to flight. Before Hepenstal could be finished off, word came that a large force from Ballinamuck were fast approaching and the rebels and their leaders had to try and make good their escape. In the retreat, dozens of rebels were captured. Most of these poor men were country farmers and labourers, not professionally trained solders.

The captives were tied hand and foot and thrown for a whole night on the streets of Granard. In the morning a number of yeomen, who had been sent out during the night to gather cattle for provisions, arrived with a drove of fat bullocks.

Without hesitation, this herd was driven over the prostrate and bound rebels until they had trampled the life out of them. After this any who still showed signs of life were handed over to Hepenstal, who had recovered from the blow he had received the previous day but had vengeance on his mind. He finished them off as fast as they were handed to him.

Hepenstal's karma finally caught up with him. While several dates for his death have been put forward, 1804 seems the most likely. He developed 'pediculosis', that is, he became infested with lice. *The Irish Magazine*, a Dublin nationalist monthly publication, reported that Hepenstal died in bed in St Andrews Street, Dublin, 'of the most shocking distemper: his body was literally devoured by vermin; and the agonies of his sufferings were aggravated by the most awful expressions, declaring the tortures of a soul apparently surrounded with all the impatient messengers of hell.'

He was buried in either St Andrews Street or the Bully's Acre in Kilmainham. *The Irish Magazine* said about his burial that 'so secretly has the spot been concealed, lest some disloyal hand should violate the valuable shrine, that no enquirer, however ingenious, could accurately say, "Here lies the Walking Gallows!"'

REFERENCES

Tales of the Wicklow Hills, pp.57–58, Richard Marsh, 2007.

Historical Notes & Stories of the Co. Longford, pp.95–99, James P. Farrell, Dollard, 1886.

www.hauntedohiobooks.com/news/a-walking-gallows

History of Pediculosis, pp.139–142, Lawrence Charles Parish, M.D.

www.countywicklowheritage.org/page/ the_wicklow_milita_-_the_terrors_of-westmeath

18

WHATEVER YOU SAY, SAY NOTHING

There was a very well-known butcher called Paul Reddy in Longford town about the year 1740. He worked and lived in the town until his death in 1763, upon which he was interred in Longford graveyard.

In addition to being well known in the locality, Paul had a reputation for the high quality of the meats he sold. Nothing but the best was good enough for him. He always took great care at markets when purchasing cattle, sheep or pigs. Before bidding or negotiating for any animal, he would examine the beast from head to toe. From his experience he was easily able to distinguish 'the wheat from the chaff'. It was this attention to detail that gained Reddy his reputation. Because he had such a reputation, he did a large and lively trade, especially with the families of all the gentry in the general area of Longford.

There was one customer, however, with whom he had a lot of trouble: an unnamed clergyman who was very bad at settling his account. This was not an occasional oversight but a regular occurrence. This annoyed Reddy greatly but as he was a 'man of the cloth' he was slow to take action. Eventually, in desperation Paul refused point blank to give his reverence any more credit. The clergyman was very upset at being treated in such a manner by a lowly tradesman.

One Sunday the clergyman was expecting some guests for lunch. He sent a servant boy to Reddy asking for a joint of beef for their dinner. He told the boy to tell Paul that if he would oblige on this occasion, he would pay all he owed in a few days.

The boy brought the message as he had been instructed. Reddy almost exploded with anger. He threw the boy out, telling the terrified servant that until his master paid what he was owed he would get no more meat.

The boy returned and when he entered the church the Sunday service was in progress. The reverend was preaching from the Epistle of St Paul to the Romans. '… And, dearly beloved brethren,' said he, 'what did Paul say?'

'He said,' answered the servant boy, mistaking the question, 'that he would give you more beef when you paid for the last.'

There was what could best be described as a 'silent gasp' from the congregation. There was a sudden silence from the preacher. Everyone present in the church understood at once the implications of what the servant boy had in all innocence said. The clergyman quickly would up his sermon and descended from the pulpit and 'there ended the lesson!'

REFERENCE

Historical Notes and Stories of the County Longford, p.149, J.P. Farrell, Dollard, Dublin, 1886.

19

POEMS AND SONGS OF 'LEO'

John Keegan Casey, a favoured son of Co. Longford, wrote many patriotic and charming verses during the nineteenth century under the nom de plume of 'Leo'. Casey was born in 1845 on the Longford–Westmeath border. His father obtained a teaching appointment in Gurteen, near Ballymahon and Kenagh. His writings later became particularly associated with Ballymahon.

The Irish Republican Brotherhood and Fenian Brotherhood were established in 1858. The IRB were a secret society and had to find a suitable place to meet to maintain this secrecy. At the time there was a priest in Ballymahon named Father Lee, the quintessential 'sagart aroon', a priest who was loved, respected by all. Fr Lee had known Casey from his boyhood. Casey applied to him to form a Purgatorian Society – a society whose aim was to pray for the souls of those in purgatory. Fr Lee gave the society his full backing. After each night's meeting, all the chairs were stacked at the back of the hall and the floor was cleared. The scholars of the Purgatorian Society were puzzled by this. They thought that if the *Dies Irae* was being chanted, the society should be seated and if the Rosary were being said then members should kneel. For both of these it made no sense to have the chairs stacked in a corner.

Gradually, the purpose became clear, while 'Leo' and his colleagues were doing good for the souls of the dead, they were also doing good for those who were living. In other words, Casey had become a Fenian organiser and this was a very safe way to find 'converts' and a drill hall. As for poor old Fr Lee, he never found

out that 'Leo' was holding Purgatorian and Fenian meetings at the same time.

It was in 1860 that Casey began writing poetry. He was first known as 'Sean the Rhymer' and as the quality of his writings and his popularity grew, he became 'Leo the Poet'. Perhaps his most well-known work is 'The Rising of the Moon', which was based on the failed 1798 rebellion around Granard.

He moved to Dublin in 1866 and it wasn't long before he became acquainted with well-known Fenians in the area where he lived. He was arrested after the Fenian Rising of 1867 and was sentenced to nine months in gaol, serving his sentence in Mountjoy Prison.

His death was both tragic and sudden. He had suffered poor health for some time with 'bad' chest and lungs, a legacy of his time in Mountjoy. However, under good medical supervision his health was improving. In March 1870 he was driving in a cab near O'Connell Bridge (Sackville Street) when he was in a collision with a dray. He tried to jump from the cab but fell badly, being concussed in the fall. The following evening, he began to vomit blood and collapsed. He was taken to his home, where he died on St Patrick's Day. He is buried in Glasnevin Cemetery.

The Rising of the Moon

'And come tell me Sean O'Farrell, tell me why you hurry so'
'Hush, mbuachaill, hush and listen,' and his cheeks were all aglow
'I bear orders from the captain, get you ready quick and soon
For the pikes must be together by the rising of the moon'

[Chorus:]
By the rising of the moon, by the rising of the moon
For the pikes must be together by the rising of the moon

'And come tell me Sean O'Farrell, where the gath'rin is to be'
'At the old spot by the river quite well known to you and me'
'One more word for signal token: whistle out the marchin' tune
With your pike upon your shoulder by the rising of the moon'

[Chorus:]
By the rising of the moon, by the rising of the moon
With your pike upon your shoulder by the rising of the moon

OUR TOASTS

Air: The Minstrel Boy
To be learned by every Longford Man
We drink a toast to the brave old land –
To the land that we love dearest;
We drink a toast to the men who stand,
Who cling to our cause the nearest

AMONG THE FLOWERS

Every name used here has reference to the neighbourhood of Ballymahon

In the leafy Tang the wild birds sang –
The brown light lay on Derry's heather;
But years have pass'd since we the last
Sat courting in the summer weather.
The tender light of stars at night,
That soothes the wanderer so weary,
Could only show the silvery glow
That lit your glance, my darling Mary!

The Inny's shore and tall Rathmore,
The sunlight on the trembling meadows,
The pastured lea by fair Lough Ree,
Are now to me but fading shadows.
Two eyes of blue still keep their hue –
Two lustrous eyes that never vary,
And on me shine with love divine –
Those eyes are thine, my darling Mary!

In summer hours, among the flowers,
The wandering west wind found thee lonely;
In autumn time the streamlet's rhyme
Appeared to chime unto thee only.
By wildwood side, by Shrughan's tide,
You wandered like a gladsome fairy –
No winds can tell the airy spell
That floated round thy presence, Mary!
O loved and lost! Tho' tempest tost,
The exile's track is mine for ever;
Far o'er the sea, astor machree,
I stray to thee Inny's river –
For by its side I'd call thee bride,
But fortune of its gifts was chary;
A sunlit gleam – a passing dream
And all is gone for ever, Mary!

References

A Wreath of Shamrocks, pp.31–33, Dublin, 1867.

https://genius.com/The-dubliners-the-rising-of-the-moon-lyrics

Historical Notes and Stories of the County Longford, pp.195–202, J.P. Farrell, 1886, Dollard, Dublin.

THE STORIES OF MRS HAGAN

These stories were taken down from Mrs Peter Hagan (70), Aughboy, Parish of Killoe, Co. Longford. Mrs Hagan was a noted storyteller in Killoe. Her maiden name was Annie Bond and she learned all her stories from her grandmother, Anne Hughes from Rhyne. Her stories were collected in 1946.

MICK NOBLE, THE MILLER'S SON

There was a miller one time and he had a son. Mick was his name. When Mick grew up, he was a fine-looking fellow and his mother, Kitty, always told him that he would surely get a lady for a wife. 'Maureen Dillon and Kathy Roche both have an eye on you,' his mother said adding, 'but they'll never get a chance of you, you'll marry a lady.'

Lord Vanmire lived nearby and he had three daughters. They used to walk by the mill dam every evening and someone told them that Mick Noble the miller had a great fancy for a lady. One evening the youngest of the Vanmires said to Mick, 'Oh, good evening Mr Noble. I believe you have a great fancy for a lady.'

'Ha,' said Mick. 'Would a hungry hen eat oats or a duck swim?'

'We are having a party next Thursday,' says she, 'and I'm inviting you to my father's house.'

Mick went home and told his old mother what had just happened. 'You told me the truth,' he said, 'I'm invited to Lord Vanmire's on Thursday.'

'All right,' said the mother, 'but I'll have to educate you to go among gentlemen.'

Without further ado she took Mick out to the barn, put a lantern up, took him out to the middle of the barn and began teaching the lad to dance.

That night, Pat Rafferty and Jim Ryan were coming home off their céilí and stood looking at the light in Noble's barn. Rafferty said to Ryan, 'They're either "coining" (forging money) or making poteen. Come over and we'll have a look.'

Over they went to the barn and Rafferty peeped through a hole in the wall. There was old Kitty sitting on a stool instructing her son. 'Now Mick,' said she, 'I'm Lady Vanmire and you must ask me to dance. Give a bow and ask me.'

Mick came over and asked his mother, 'Lady Vanmire', for the dance. He said, 'Will you have "Father Jack Walshe?"'

'Oh no, I'll have "Miss McCleod's Reel" instead – that would be no dance for a young lady.'

Mick and his mother began dancing and, to say the least, Mick wasn't exactly light on his feet. Sometimes he'd have two left feet, the next instant he'd have two right ones. Rafferty outside fell to the ground with the laughing and Ryan had to practically carry him home.

Thursday came, and Mick got ready. Old Kitty made him wash his face in hot water to make him look white. She also wouldn't let him eat much in case he would be 'rifting' at the table in the manor house. She gave him three steps (she walked three steps with him to bring him good luck, this was a custom in the area).

Mick arrived at the Lord Vanmire's house and a waiter met him and put him sitting in a room. There he sat and sometimes a lady would come and peep at him and sometimes it was a gentleman peeper. Lady Vanmire asked the daughters why he had been invited and they said he had been invited for fun; the house was always so very dull.

After a long time, the waiter came in and told Mick he should leave as Lord Vanmire had gone away and there was to be no party.

Off he started home, feeling very dejected. When old Kitty, his mother, saw him coming back to the mill she ran to meet him. 'Mick,' said she, 'how did you do?'

Mick said, 'I was only brought to give them a laugh at my expense.'

The mother did what all mothers do. She gave Mick a big hug and held him to her. 'I'm so sorry,' said she. 'Never mind my old talk about marrying a lady. Marry a good country girl who will treat you right. Get one who can make boxty and potato bread because these ladies are far too uppish and proud.'

'No Mother,' said Mick firmly, 'unless I get a lady, I'll stay the way I am.'

So that's why there are so many old maids and old bachelors, all of them looking for something they never can get.

THE HAPPY MAN'S SHIRT

There was once a very wealthy gentleman and he got uneasy in mind and couldn't rest on account of all his wealth. He was told to get a 'happy man's shirt' and that then he could sleep. He called his steward and told him to go and find him a happy man's shirt.

The steward went to a very successful shopkeeper. The shopkeeper told him that he was indeed prosperous. 'I'm sure then you're happy,' said the steward.

'Indeed, I'm not,' said he, 'I can't rest for thinking about all the money that I'm owed.' The steward left the shopkeeper and travelled on until he met a 'strong' farmer. The steward said to the farmer's wife, 'You appear to be quite happy here.'

She answered, 'No, for I don't know when my son will bring a villain of a wife that I don't want here. I can't sleep at night on account of worrying about it.'

The steward left the farm and continued along the road. As he walked, he saw a fellow in a field, stripped to the waist becasue of the heat, turning the land with a loy (a narrow spade), and he was whistling and singing as he worked.

'You seem happy,' said the steward.

'I am indeed,' said the labourer. 'Nothing troubles me. I can spend my wages any way I like.'

'Have you nothing to annoy you?'

'Not a thing,' said the lad proudly. 'Well,' said the steward, 'I'll give you twenty pounds for your shirt.'

'You won't,' said the lad. 'For I don't even have a shirt to put on my back.'

The steward went back to his master and told him that the happiest man hadn't even a shirt on his back. A contented mind is a continual feast.

LITTLE BAD LUCK

There were two brothers, John and Peter, who lived beside each other. John had eight acres of land and Peter four. John, even with his eight acres, was envious of Peter and wanted him to leave his farm so that he could have all twelve acres for himself. He was encouraged in his envy by his wife, who begrudged anyone who had something she wanted.

Then, without warning, Peter hit trouble shortly after he had married. They were plagued by bad luck. It was one trouble after another, morning, noon and night. There seemed no end to their misfortunes. He was coming along the road home one day when he got a feeling that something was following him. He turned and saw what looked like a little maneen about the size of a hen.

'In the name of God what are you?' says Peter.

'I'm Bad Luck and I've been following you since the day you got married.'

'Faith, then you'll follow me no longer,' says he.

He caught the little fellow and tied him hand and foot. He then dug a hole with his loy and buried him. When he had finished, he said out loud, 'Thank God.'

As he walked home, he was whistling and had a smile on his face, not what you would expect from someone who always had misfortune.

John's wife said to her husband, 'Peter must have got something good. I'll go over and see what it is.'

She got a big bit of butter and a big jug of creamy milk and went over to Peter's cottage. When John's wife handed over the butter and milk, Peter's wife said, 'Thanks be to God, that's the first bit of good luck we've had for a long, long time.'

'I heard you whistling as you came back the road earlier and you looked in very good form. What did you get?' asked John's wife casually.

Peter's wife then told her of the experience Peter had with the little maneen, Bad Luck. John's wife said she didn't believe her, not for a second.

The following morning, she was at her window before day-break to see what was happening at the other household. Peter left for his work and she followed him. When Peter came to the spot where he had buried Bad Luck, he lifted the flagstone over the hole. Sure enough, Bad Luck was still there. Peter replaced the flag and went on about his business. When he had dis-appeared around a bend in the road, John's wife came over and lifted the flag. She looked in and sure enough there was the little fellow in the pit just as had been described to her the day before.

She released the little maneen and told him to follow Peter as he normally did. 'I won't,' said Bad Luck, 'but I'll follow yourself.'

She tried to catch him with the intention of putting him back into the pit. However, Bad Luck was too nimble for her, he dodged her lunge and disappeared in an instant.

When she went back home, one of her husband John's cows was lying in the field near the house stone dead. Every week after that some other misfortune befell John and his wife. It wasn't long before everything was gone, and they had nothing. At the same time, Peter and his wife began to flourish. Eventually, John and his wife were forced by their circumstances to sell their eight acres to Peter and his good wife and leave the area for good.

Leave envy alone and it will punish itself.

THE LITTLE SHOEMAKER

Long ago and long ago it was, there was a little shoemaker called Paddy. Paddy used to make boots, bring them to town and sell them. One day after selling his boots he went on a spree, wasted the price of his boots and hadn't a penny piece left. He had to go to the leather merchant and beg the makings of two pairs of boots as all his money was gone. The leather merchant, being a decent man, gave Paddy the makings of two pairs.

When he got home his wife said, 'You brought two pairs with you and brought home the makings of two more, how much profit did you make?'

Paddy had to think of an answer quickly and said, 'No profit, the price of leather had gone up something terrible.'

His wife, guessing what had really happened, said, 'Well so have the price of provisions gone up. You'll get no dinner in this house tonight.'

Paddy took the leather out to his workshop and left it on the bench. As there was going to be no dinner he went back into the house and went straight to bed.

He got up the next morning and went to the workshop to make the boots. When he entered the workshop, there on the bench were two lovely pairs of shoes, the best he had ever laid eyes on. While he had no idea how they came to be there, he tied them up and went off to town to sell them. Before he sold them, he called on the leather merchant and the foreman said, 'Paddy, I've never seen anyone improve so much in the quality of their work.'

Paddy said nothing, but the foreman went off and got him the makings of six pairs. Paddy sold the two pairs and headed for home. He left the makings in his workshop and went off on his céilí.

Next morning when he went out to the workshop there were six more pairs of the finest shoes money could buy. Paddy opened up his own boot and shoe shop. He was getting on so well that his wife was getting very uneasy to see who was actually making the footwear. She could see that the quality was beyond anything her husband could produce. She questioned Paddy, whose only answer was, 'What loss, as long as they are made.'

The next night the wife went out to the workshop to see who was making the boots and shoes. She fell asleep despite her best efforts to stay awake. She saw nothing but, in the morning, there was a new supply of the beautiful boots and shoes. The following night she fixed up a screen in the corner of the shop and determined that she wouldn't fall asleep again. After eleven o'clock in came two fairies with a hammer and a last each. By two o'clock in the morning they had a whole range of footwear completed. Paddy's wife couldn't believe what she was seeing.

The two little fairies picked up their hammers and lasts and pointed the lasts towards the corner where the wife was hiding. Each fairy let out a hearty laugh and out they went. The next morning the wife was blind, as blind as a bat. Paddy was less than sympathetic to his wife's condition. 'Maybe now you're satisfied,' he said.

That night Paddy, as had become routine, left a fresh supply of leather in the workshop. When he came back the next morning there was the leather just as he had left it. Neither boots nor shoes had been made. The fairy shoemakers never came back. All the money that Paddy had made flew away from him quicker than it had come, and they were destitute once more.

After that Paddy said that it was always better to let hidden things remain hidden.

Reference

NFC 1498, 98–99, 100–101, 127–130, Mrs Peter Hagan (70), Aughaboy, Killoe, Co. Longford, March 1946.

21

THE CORLEA
TRACKWAY

In the bog land three kilometres west of Keenagh in south Co. Longford generations of local turf-cutters have spoken of a 'Danes Road', which lay about two metres below the surface of the raised bog. Often when they were cutting turf, they would come upon oak beams that seemed to be part of some roadway or 'togher'. Little was made of this and it was just regarded as a feature of the bog in the area.

Then, in 1984, when Bord na Móna were engaged in mechanical 'harvesting' of turf in the area, they uncovered a prehistoric road or trackway made of oak beams. This roadway, it was later learned, had nothing to do with the 'Danes' or Vikings. It was in fact a much older structure dating back to pre-Christian times. It was a very substantial construction and much stronger than other wattle and brush paths that had often been discovered in the bog.

Samples of the oak beams of the roadway were carbon dated as belonging to trees that had been felled in 147 or 148 BC. This was an amazing discovery and a major archaeological excavation was started under the direction of Professor Barry Raftery. The work continued until 1991 before the site was destroyed by the mechanical turf harvesting. Fortunately, an eighteen-metre section of the trackway was preserved in a purpose-built, climate-controlled building that prevented the ancient timbers from decomposing. This building became the Corlea Trackway Visitor Centre and was made accessible to the public.

Today the area looks like wasteland; brown, flat with no features to break up the billiard-table-like appearance of the landscape. It would not always have been like this. During the Iron Age much of Ireland was covered by bog lands. These soggy wetlands were made up of partly decomposed dead plants, flowers and trees. At the end of the last Ice Age more than ten thousand years ago much of the land was flooded by the melting ice. Poor drainage would have left large areas of wet land, into which decaying material fell. These were dangerous places and totally impassable for parts of the year when the weather was wettest. The surrounding area was covered by dense forests of hazel, willow and birch. Ash and oak would have covered the higher ground.

Because of the conditions of the soil in these wetlands and the lack of oxygen, the dead plant life would have only partially decayed. This in time became turf. The anaerobic (lacking in oxygen) nature of the bogs preserved the timbers of the trackway until they were discovered in 1984.

The Corlea Trackway runs for about one kilometre into the bog to a small area of dry ground. It is made in a style known as a 'corduroy road'. This corduroy pattern was of split oak beams between three and three and a half metres wide and about fifteen

centimetres thick, laid on rails of birch. The birch rails were set about a metre apart. This would have been an enormous feat of construction. Professor Raftery estimated that it would have required three hundred oak trees. These trees would have needed to be felled, de-branched and split along their grain by hammering in wedges. As the trees began to split, wider and wider wedges would have been used until the mighty oak finally split. It is estimated that more than a thousand wagon loads of these beams would have been needed to be transported to the site and then carried manually to their position on the trackway. Holes were made in the oak beams and stakes hammered into the bog below to hold them in place.

While other trackways of simple woven hurdles laid on heaped brushwood suitable for people to walk on were discovered in the area, nothing as substantial as the main trackway existed. Similar trackways have been found in Germany, the Netherlands and Britain but none compare to Corlea, which is bigger and heavier than any other prehistoric road in Europe. It would have been an immense undertaking, requiring the work of an unbelievable number of men.

One of the most extraordinary features of the Corlea Trackway is that it seems to have been built without purpose and simply leads into the bog. In fact, the roadway didn't last more than about fifteen years at most as it simply sank under its own weight below the surface of the bog until it was rediscovered in 1984. For something so substantial and requiring such effort it would seem to be a purposeless endeavour.

So why was the trackway here in the first place? It seems to just begin and end as if it were a project started but unfinished. Many questions, few answers.

REFERENCES

https://www.discoverireland.ie/Arts-Culture-Heritage/
    corlea-trackway-visitor-centre/582
www.megalithicireland.com/Corlea%20Trackway.html
www.ancientireland.org/corlea
www.heritageireland.ie/en/midlands-eastcoast/
    corleatrackwayvisitorcentre

22

MORGAN FINN

This story was collected from James Farrell, who was born in 1867. James was living in Furze, Lenamore, Rathreagh, Co. Longford. He was born in Carrickboy, Kilglass, which was amalgamated with Rathreagh and Augharra to form the parish of Legan. Most of his stories he heard from his father, who was born in 1836 and who died in 1926. This story was collected in May 1955.

There was once a widow who had one son, Morgan Finn. He never got out of bed. He just lay and grew and grew until his feet reached to the door. His mother fed him on roasted potatoes and goat's milk. She had a terrible time trying to satisfy his hunger. One day, Morgan decided he had had enough of the bed and made up his mind to go and seek his fortune.

His mother bought a 'web' of frieze to make a coat for him. She put two pockets in the coat that were so big that they reached down to the ground. When the coat was finished, she made five hundredweight of oatmeal into oaten bread for him. She then put another five hundredweight of meal into the pockets and off he started.

He travelled along until he came to a clear stream. He began to feel both hungry and thirsty. He went down to the stream and he'd throw a handful of the oaten meal into the stream and catch it in his mouth as it flowed down to him. While he was at this, a man came along and asked him what he was doing. Morgan said he was out to seek his fortune. The man gave him a key as a token and directed him to a big house nearby and said he'd be sure to get work there. Morgan thanked the man and set off towards the big house. When he got to the house, he asked to see the gentleman of the house. The gentleman came, and Morgan showed him the key and said he wanted work. He was employed and sent into the kitchen to get his dinner. There were twenty men employed in the place and their dinners were on the table ready for them. Morgan laid into them and ate them all.

When his master heard this news, he was in a terrible rage and sent for his Grand Advisor. She said that he was to put Morgan to thrash fifteen big stacks of oats that were in the haggard or be beheaded if he didn't finish the job in a day. The master went to Morgan and gave him his orders. He handed him a flail, but Morgan just laughed and said that the flail was no good, that it was only a 'cipín' (little stick). He ordered that five hundredweight of iron be made into a 'hand staff' and three hundredweight into a 'buailtín' (pounder). The master told Morgan to yoke up a horse and to cart the iron to the forge. Morgan didn't bother yoking the horse he just carried the iron to the forge himself and had the flail made. He returned to the haggard and attacked the stacks with the flail and hammered the whole lot into chaff in less than a day.

The Grand Advisor was called again. She said to send Morgan down to the bull that was in the field and that he'd surely be killed, for the bull was so wicked that no one ever returned if they ventured into that field. Morgan was told to go down and get the bull. Off he started with his flail under his arm. When he reached the field, he saw the bull on the side of a hill. As soon as the bull saw him, he charged at full speed. Morgan thanked the bull for coming to him so quickly and saving him a long walk. The bull horned him and Morgan became very angry. He struck the bull with the flail and cut it into two halves.

He threw the flail over his shoulder and, taking a half of the bull in each hand, walked away home. On the way, a hare jumped up right at his feet. He threw half the bull at the hare and killed her. He picked up the dead hare, the half bull and continued home. When he reached the house, the master asked him what the hare was, and Morgan said it was the bull's calf. The master said he'd take the hare. Morgan lit a fire, roasted both halves of the bull and ate the lot.

By this time the master was growing afraid of Morgan, so he went again to the Grand Advisor and asked her what he should do next. She told him to send Morgan to hell for the master's father and to bring him back home with him. Morgan got his orders to go to hell for the old man, but he asked how would he recognise the father? The master said he'd find him standing inside the door wearing a three-cornered hat. Off Morgan went to hell and when he got there, he demanded to see the old man. They handed him out. Morgan brought him home and shut him up in the barn. He went into the house and said he had the old man outside. As soon as he said that he was ordered to take him back to hell immediately. This he did.

The next day the Grand Advisor was again consulted. She said to send Morgan to plough the park along the seashore. No one ever returned from this area because sea monsters came up and devoured both men and horses. Morgan started down to the field on the seashore and began to plough. He wasn't long there until a sea monster came up and took one of the horses into the sea and devoured it. The monster came up again, but Morgan captured it and yoked it to the plough and made it plough the whole field. When evening came and the ploughing was finished, Morgan brought the sea monster back to the house.

The next day the very frightened master went to the Grand Advisor and asked yet again was there anything they could do to get rid of Morgan. She said to send him over to the giant's castle and order him to strip the slates off the roof. When morning came, he yoked the sea monster to a boat and loaded it with ladders and tools. He arrived at the castle before the giant was awake. Morgan got up on the roof and began smashing away. On hearing the noise, out rushed the giant and ordered him down. Morgan paid no heed to the giant and kept on smashing. The giant threw up the boat at Morgan, but Morgan just caught it and flung it back down, killing the giant.

Out came another giant with two heads and he threw a big rock up at Morgan. Again, Morgan simply caught the rock and threw it back, killing the second giant. Then another giant with three heads came out of the castle and he was in such a rage that he ran up the ladder to get at Morgan. Morgan struck him one mighty blow and knocked off all three heads.

Morgan piled the slates on the boat and threw the three dead giants up on top of the slates and brought them home. The master had to have the giants buried. By this stage, the master was in such fear of Morgan that he gave him his house and his daughter as his wife and quickly went to live in another place himself.

So, they made brogues out of slippers and slippers out of glass and all came sliding home on their ass!

REFERENCE

NFC 1498, 139–145, James Farrell (88), Lenamore, Co. Longford. Jim Delaney, May 1955.

23

THE SHERIFF'S SEIZURES

This account is from Patrick Reilly (76) from Enaghan, Dromard, Co. Longford. Patrick heard it fifty years earlier from his grand uncle, who was aged 70 and also lived in Enaghan. The story was told in the first person. It has such an immediacy that it could have been told today. For that reason, it is presented exactly as Patrick told it. The collector Jim Delaney has added some notes for clarification to the text.

I seen several seizures and attempted seizures and seen a rescue of stock that was taken. Five men took part in the rescue, they were Mick McNaboe, Francie the Mill's cousin, three Reillys, John, Edward Bawn and John's son, Eddie, and a neighbour Mick Pháid.

This was the time that the land was going to be bought out by the tenants and the arrangements were partly med [made]. There was a 'hanging gale' [a half-year's rent that was always in advance] and no matter how much you paid you always had this hanging gale to pay. It was always there. I don't rightly know why it was there. Then there was another thing, something about a year's rent to be added to the purchase money. The tenants were fightin' about them two things, fightin' to get rid of the extra year's purchase money and the hangin' gale.

So, the tenants around here let the rent get behind purposely. I was in it meself, though I was only young at the time, between man and boy. So, the decree was out for many in this townland including us. This townland [Enaghan, JD] was isolated from other townlands because it was a Charles McConkey who owned it and he had no other land about but it.

We were all worked up to such an extent that we were out day and night watchin' for the Sheriff, so we could drive our cattle to a neighbour's place, who had their rent paid. There was a man Hugh Reilly who lived on the north side of McNaboe's mill and he was tired watchin' for the Sheriff. The Sheriff was so long comin' that we all began to get slack.

One mornin' I was in bed and I heard a terrible shout that the Sheriff was comin'. I got out of bed and with only me trousers on I ran out and grabbed the first thing that came to me hand. It was a 'grape' [a type of fork]. I never considered meself much of a fightin' man or anything like that, but I was ready for war that day. I stood before the byre dure [door] with the grape. Next door, the father and son was also out prepared.

This Hugh Reilly, he had céilíed late and was comin' home about the Castle Hill and didn't he see the Sheriff comin'. He started for home as fast as he could and rooted out his brother, Frank. Frank pulled on his trousers. Hugh took for Upper and Frank for Lower Enaghan to give the alarm. Hugh riz [rose] them in one place and Frank in the other.

A man lived in Longford the name of Real [Rehill or Reehill is the correct spelling, JD]. He had a post car and he brought out the Sheriff in his car. Real could see Frank runnin' from one house to other and he held in the horse. The Sheriff was goin' to strike the horse for not goin' fast enough but Real stopped him. 'You hired me to bring you out here and I'm doin' it,' he says to the Sheriff, 'but don't you lave [leave] a finger on that horse. He's tired and can go no faster.'

Any of the cattle that was loose the Sheriff took but lucky for me and the Murthaghs [next-door neighbours, JD] didn't the Sheriff meet four of them five lads I toule [told] you about in the beginnin', Mick McNaboe, John and Edward Bán Reilly and Mick Phaid. They took the cattle off the Sheriff and drove them all over the country. Eddie Reilly, John's son, took a mare they had. The mare was in the stable and the Sheriff and his men come to take it. Eddie got up on the mare's back and waited for them to open the stable dures [doors]. When they did, he galloped out the mare and knocked the Sheriff and his men left and right and away with him across the country. So, the Sheriff got nothin' for his trouble.

I drove pigs we had to Masterson's house and left them there. I was only a runner at the time – between a gossun and a man. I went into Arva to hear what I could after all the fuss was over. The Sheriff was in the Barracks and had sworn agin' [against] the five men. Sergeant Connolly was in Arva Barracks that time and he was a very dacent man. He comes up the town and enquired if there was anyone from Enaghan there. Someone told him that I was from Enaghan and he comes to me and toule [told] me that information was sworn agin' five men from Enaghan and says he to me, 'Do you know them?'

'I know them well,' I says.

'If I go up to Enaghan now,' he says, 'none of them men will appear. Will you contact them and tell them I'll be in Mick McNaboe's in an hour. They can meet me there if they wish. If they don't, some night we'll take them off their beds. We'll get them sometime.'

So back I went to Enaghan and I heard

that the five lads were out on the Lough. I whistled, and they come in and I told them the message the sergeant gave me.

'Well,' says auld John Ban, 'we may as well go and face it, or we'll be on the run the rest of our lives.'

Some of them was agin' that but at last they all decided to go to Mick McNaboe's.

Mick's mother was in the field and meself and John Bán goin' up to the house. 'Come here Patrick,' she says to me when she heard the news. 'You seem to have the ear of the sergeant. I wonder could you get him to take auld Mick [her husband] and leave young Michael with me?'

'I couldn't do the like, ma'am,' says I, 'and I don't know the sergeant at all. I was only in Arva today and someone told him I was from Enaghan and he tould me to bring the message.'

'Well,' says auld John Bawn, 'did anyone ever hear the like. The auld vagaonbone, that's all she thinks of, her man!'

Anyway, the five boys met the sergeant in McNaboe's and them all started for Arva and the 'weight' of the townland with them along the road. There was a Father Edward Mahon in Columcille that time. He was a peculiar, odd sort of man but he had so much influence he'd take you from the gallows. He happened to drive into Arva the same day in his horse and trap. Someone told him what was after happenin' in Enaghan that day. He left the trap in town and walked out and met them all on the road and shook hands with the five men.

The case was brought agin' the men for interferin' with the Sheriff. In the meantime, the arrangements were started for to buy the land and them all were let off on the First Offenders Act.

REFERENCE

NFC 1457, 42–47, Patrick Reilly (76), Enaghan, Dromard, Co. Longford. Jim Delaney.

24

THE GRAVE DIGGER

This story was given to me by Vincent Pierce, Ballymurray, who was given it by another lad he often met at storytelling sessions and similar gatherings. He couldn't recall the lad's name so the best I can do is give the pedigree of from whom I heard the story.

There was a young man, John Farrell, and he was living just outside Carrickboy. The poor boy had come from a broken home with no one to guide him in the right direction. As a result, he received little or no education. He was working for farmers picking stones, splitting timber and bringing in loads of turf, all that sort of work. He was getting very little reward for all his hard labour.

All this was happening when emigration from all over the country as well as Co. Longford was running at a very high level. They were leaving Ireland by the thousand. Now living beside this young man was a neighbour who was very fond of him because he knew him to be a very good worker and a very honest lad. One evening he met him on his way home from work and he said, 'John, if you stay round here working for farmers, you'll never have anything. Now, there are two sons of mine over in London and they're earning good money. My third lad is going over in a couple of weeks' time to join them. If I was you, I'd travel over with him. I'll drop a line to my eldest lad, and I'll tell him to be on the lookout for a job for you and a place to stay. Have a think about it.'

'God,' said John, 'that would be great.'

Anyway, to cut a long story short, he went to London. He got a job with 'The Green Murphy', civil engineers, and he was staying in a place called Willesden. Every morning at a quarter past seven he had to get up on the back of a lorry with a lot of other lads, mostly from all over Ireland, and they were driven out to the country to the building site. He spent the whole day diggin' trenches. Five days, six days, sometimes seven days of the week. He'd be dropped back in the evenings at about a quarter to six and he'd go into the café and have his dinner. Sometimes if he was in the form, he might go into the Spotty Dog pub and have a pint or two.

The barman in the Spotty Dog noticed that John was always sitting on his own, he seemed to have no friends. One evening the barman was out collecting glasses and he got chatting to him. The barman asked him where he was from.

'I'm from Co. Longford in Ireland just outside a little place called Carrickboy.'

'How long are you over here in London?' enquired the barman.

'I'm here about seven or eight months,' answered John, 'but I don't like it at all. I've no friends and I'm spending all my days digging trenches. I don't know what's happening back home. I don't know who's winnin' the matches, I don't know anything.'

The barman said to him, 'Why don't you get the Longford paper; I think it's called the *Longford Leader*. They sell all the Irish papers in the newsagent's just down the road outside on the left.'

'Ah,' said John, 'that's my problem. I can't read nor write.'

'Oh,' said the barman sympathetically, 'I'm very sorry to hear that, very sorry. But I'll tell you what I'll do. There's a man from Longford who comes in here every Thursday evening, he sits over there, and he reads the *Longford Leader* from cover to cover. I'll introduce you to him and you can meet him every Thursday evening and you can have a chat about what's going on in your home place.'

'God,' said John, 'that'd be great.'

The following Thursday, John came into the pub and sure enough the man with the *Longford Leader* was there in his usual spot. The barman introduced the two men and they got on well, the old and the young. From then on, every Thursday they'd meet but John was still always going on about home and how homesick he was. One evening the man was going through the paper and he said to John, 'There's a job here that would suit you down to the ground.'

'What is it?' asked John.

'Longford County Council are looking for a grave digger. Wouldn't you be well able to do that?'

'Be dad I would,' said John, 'I'm digging trenches every day of the week for the last ten months. I'm as fit as a fiddle and diggin' three or four graves would be no problem.'

'Well,' said his friend, 'if I were you, I'd go back to Longford and apply for the job because if you're not happy in a job, there's no point in staying in it.'

So, that's what John did. He came back to Longford, into the council office and the girl showed him up to the office where the man who was dealing with that job was. He sat him down and they had a good long chat and what experience he had.

'I've been working for the "Green Murphy" in England for nearly a year, diggin' trenches every day, five, six and seven days a week sometimes. I'd have no trouble digging three or four graves.'

The council official said that was great and that he seemed like a very highly suitable applicant for the job.

'Now,' said the official, 'there are three or four other people interested in it, but what I'll do is, if you just fill in this application form here, I'll be in touch with you within the next week or two.'

He handed him the form and a biro. The young fellow said, 'That's my problem, I can't read or write.'

'Oh,' said the council man, 'well if you can't read or write, I can't give you the job.'

'And what does reading and writing got to do with diggin' graves?' demanded John.

'Well it does,' said the official, 'we have to keep a logbook, fill the date of the funeral, the time of the funeral all that sort of thing. It's very important, we have to keep a record of the whole thing. I'm very sorry but I can't give you the job.'

John left the council offices in very bad form and very frustrated. He had a good deal of money saved up and he knew there was a cousin of his going to America. He approached him and said, 'I hear you're going to America, next month.'

'That's right,' said the cousin.

'Would you mind if I travelled with you?' enquired John.'

'No, problem, you'd be very welcome, and I'd enjoy your company.'

So off John and his cousin headed for America the following month. The story doesn't shed any light on what work John was doing in America but ten years later he returned to his native Longford a multimillionaire. He decided he'd invest his money in one of the big banks in Dublin, so nobody would know his business. This would have been way back in the 1960s when Ireland was a very small place in terms of people knowing your business. Off he headed for Dublin.

When he got there, he went into one of the big banks and asked the girl behind the counter, 'What interest rates are you paying?'

'Well,' the girl said, 'it depends on how much you have to invest; the more money, the better the rate.' John calmly answered, 'Well, I have seven and a half million.'

'Oh, my God!' said the shocked girl. 'Can you take a seat there for a minute? I'll have to have a word with the manager.'

She phoned the manager and explained. The manager said to her on the phone, 'Get that man a cup of tea or a drink but don't let him out of the bank. Bring him up here to my office, we can't lose a potentially good customer like him.'

The girl did as she had been instructed and brought John up to the manager's office. They sat down, and they had a good long chat. When they had settled everything about an hour and a half later, the manager handed him the form to fill in and sign and a pen to sign it with.

John said, 'That's my problem, I can neither read nor write.'

'What do you mean,' asked the bank manager, 'can't read or write?'

'I can't read nor write,' said John.

'And you've come back from America,' the shocked manager said, 'with seven and a half million. Good God man, seven and a half million pounds and you can't read nor write. Just what could you have been if you had been able to read and write?'

'A grave digger for Longford County Council,' answered John with a smile.

25

THE REJECTED CUB
OF THE FAIRIES

One moonlit night in either the year 1845 or the spring of 1846 the people on the eastern side of Drumhalry heard a great battle in progress. What was extraordinary about this battle was that it was between armies of invisible beings. The rush and roar of the conflict was savage, and the shouts of the combatants was clear, even though they remained invisible.

As the noises began and grew in volume and savagery, the neighbours all began to come out of their cottages to listen to what was going on. The noise started early on the moonlit night and continued for well over an hour. Needless to say, neighbours were asking each other what was going on, as no obvious explanation of the phenomenon was evident. Neither was it possible to tell whether the battle had resulted in a truce, a defeat or a win for one side.

The farmer whose residence appeared to be closest to the conflict was Jimmy Reilly, known to all as 'Jimmy the Bull'. Reilly normally kept a bull on his land. In saying that his farm was nearest the conflict, it was hard to exactly place the location, but it was in his area that the sounds were at their loudest and most terrible.

When the noise of battle faded, a terrible silence hung over the area. One by one the families began to return to their cottages discussing what they had just witnessed, if indeed 'witness' is the correct word for something heard but not seen.

Like all the others, the Reilly family retired to their dwelling, but their son, young Jimmy, could not be found. They searched high up and low down but could find no trace of the youth.

Members of the Reilly family called on every house in the area, but nobody had seen young Jimmy during the spectacle that had just taken place.

Jimmy was a young man of about eighteen years. He was tall, upright and good looking. The family grew more frantic as the evening and then the night wore on. Finally, around midnight, Jimmy was found asleep among the hay in Reilly's own barn. Naturally there was great relief among them that Jimmy was safe from harm. His family had great difficulty in waking him but awaken he did eventually. When the lad stood up there was a

hump on his back, which he carried all the days of his life from that moment on.

The big question all the Reillys had was, 'Where was young Jimmy all evening?' Their own barn was one of the first places they had searched when they began looking for him but at that stage there had been no sign of him. Jimmy had no recollection of the evening nor the events all others in the district had heard. Why had this tall, straight and erect young man suddenly become crippled in the space of one evening? Was there a connection between the noisy tumult the people heard and Jimmy's problems? No one could say. It wasn't long before theories about both events began to circulate around the area.

The fact that Jimmy had seemingly become as invisible as the noisy fighters could mean only one thing: Jimmy had been taken by the fairies. What of the hump on his back? The clear explanation of this was that for some reason better known to themselves the fairies had rejected Jimmy. From that time on Jimmy became known as 'the rejected cub of the fairies'.

Life despite his deformity seemed to be working out well for Jimmy. He eventually married, and he was blessed with two children. However, he died young. By the time of his death the children had grown into good-looking young people. Jimmy's wife remarried, as was the custom of the time. A widow with young children needed to remarry in order to survive. The woman had two more children for her second husband. The extraordinary feature of these two children was that they looked much more like the late Jimmy than they did their own father. This was noticed by all but never commented upon.

Reference

NFC 656, 29, Patrick Duffy, Drumhalry, Co. Longford. Séamus Ó Duileargy, August 1935.

26

LAND WAR IN
DRUMLISH, 1881

'The Land War', as it was known, was a period in Ireland of the 1870s–90s when there was agitation among tenant farmers over their rights or lack of them. Many tenant farmers had no right to written leases. When a rental agreement, usually for a period of twelve months, ended, they could be evicted. The Land League was formed as a popular movement to obtain what became known as the '3Fs' – free sale, fixity of tenure and fair rent.

Many folk tales have emerged from the struggle of individuals and communities at this difficult time. No tales of this period could be more famous than the Land War in Drumlish. Its hero, the parish priest Fr Tom Conefry, lives on in the folk memory of the area to the present day.

The Great Famine of the 1840s had savaged the population, especially in areas where land quality was very poor. However, during the 1850s and '60s farm prices and earnings had been good. This led farmers to agree to higher rents. All this changed in the 1870s when all over Europe there were low prices, bad weather and poor harvests in what became known as the 'Long Depression'. Wheat was imported from the United States and refrigerated meat from Argentina and Australia, which kept prices for home-produced goods low.

By the 1880s things had reached breaking point. It was against this background that the Land War of Drumlish took place. For seven months during 1880, three hundred families in the parish of Drumlish were supported by 'alms' from the public, organised and collected by the parish priest, Fr Tom Conefry. In his first appeal Fr Conefry said:

> There are many houses in this parish at present in which the last pound of meal has been consumed; the last bed covering worth a shilling has been deposited in the pawn-office, and the last fire of turf collected from the saturated heap upon the bog has died away from the hearth, the dying embers being a vivid emblem of that death from starvation which is already creeping upon the threshold.

Only through the never-flagging efforts of Fr Conefry had famine been averted in the Drumlish area. The harvest of autumn 1880, grown with seeds begged for by Fr Conefry and his curate Fr William Gray, had been saved and stored. Now having dodged the famine's bullet in 1880 the tenants were being expected to sell their oats and potatoes to pay their rents in 1881.

On the night of 11 January 1881, people were roused from their sleep by messengers with word the dreaded bailiff was coming the following day to serve 'processes' for rack-rents. The people of Drumlish and Ballinamuck were quickly out of their beds to make ready to prevent the process server from carrying out his task. Land League drums and the ringing of church bells warned every man, woman and child of the impending danger of eviction. On the morning of 12 January, groups began to gather in each townland of the parish. The general view of every man in the parish was that, 'We will die fighting like men sooner than allow any rack-renter rob us of the food necessary for ourselves and our families. It is better for us to die fighting like soldiers, than die of starvation like slaves.'

A crowd gathered in Drumlish along with a crowd from Ballinamuck, followed by more people from all over the parish. The cry went up, 'The process server is coming.' The crowd, which would have been a mob only for the settling influence

of Fr Conefry, who was proving to be a tireless leader, met the bailiff on the outskirts of the village approaching from Newtownforbes, guarded by a small force of Royal Irish Constabulary (RIC). The RIC were not prepared for this reception, so they quickly fixed bayonets and formed a hollow square around the process server.

The process server stated that he had no 'processes' with him. Someone handed him a Bible and made him swear that he was telling the truth. Having done so, the party was allowed to proceed to Drumlish barracks. As soon as they were safely in the barracks a telegram was sent to Longford town calling for reinforcements.

A force of eighty-five police under Resident Magistrate Rogers and District Inspector Horne rushed towards Drumlish. When they arrived, they formed a larger hollow square around the unfortunate process server, who was trembling with fear. This force then headed towards the home of Thomas Rogers in the townland of Derawley, who was first on the list of 'victims'. The crowd rushed ahead of the police and by the time they arrived at Rogers' home it was surrounded by a crowd of about three thousand, all armed with whatever was available to them: forks, scythes, sickles, sticks. The RM read the Riot Act. The crowd refused to move.

The RM was an experienced military man as well as being a man of some humanity. After a stand-off he ordered the police to retire to the Drumlish barracks. Their return to Drumlish was not a pleasant journey for them; they were crowded, jeered and insulted by the following mob of angry men and women. The RM told the people that he would return the following day with reinforcements and complete his task.

Throughout the night of 12 January there was an extraordinary level of activity around the whole parish. The church bell was rung, horns blew, and drums were played. All the while, more and more people headed towards the village. Fr Conefry was again tireless that night. He sent word to his bishop to intercede with Lord Granard to prevent carnage the following day. Lord Granard's reply to the bishop stated that there was 'no danger of a collision between the people and the police in Drumlish. Tomorrow I'll send dragoons that will soon restore and keep order.' The stage was set for a potential disaster.

The next morning cars were arriving in the village by the dozen, all full of police from every station throughout the district. As each cart or carload of police arrived at the barracks they were met with a hail of stones and had to rush inside. Five Resident Magistrates arrived with the police as well as all officer ranks within the police – sub-inspectors, county inspectors and district inspectors.

The build-up of people continued in the village. As J.P.
Farrell stated, 'They came from all directions. A common
cause to fight landlordism brought them from all the neigh-
bouring parishes, from Killoe, Clonbroney, Columbkille,
Drumard, Cloone, Aughavas, Gortitteragh, Bornacoola,
Cloonguidh, etc.'

The people were not a mob but were operating in a very
disciplined manner. They advanced on the barracks, where by
morning there were five hundred police. The crowd were chant-
ing, 'We defy all the police in the barracks to serve a process.
Down with rack-rents. Down with Landlordism. We will die
fighting like men and not die of starvation.'

Once more Fr Conefry was to the fore. He feared that the
crowd would attack the barracks and that there would be
extensive bloodshed on both sides. The leaders agreed not to
attack but only so long as the process server didn't attempt to
serve a process. At about eleven o'clock word came that about
a hundred and fifty dragoons had been seen approaching in the
distance. They arrived in the village at a smart trop and took up
battle formation about two hundred yards from the crowd.

The crowd's blood was up. They shouted, 'Come on with
your swords if you dare. If you have swords, we have pitchforks
and scythes, and for every slash of a sword you give one of us we
will give ten strokes of a scythe in return.'

The crowd then turned to the hollow square of five hundred
policemen with the process server in the centre and said, 'Come
on now if you dare, we defy you.'

Tension between the opposing forces couldn't have been
higher, all that would be needed for a disaster would be one
wrong action on either side. Fr Conefry, who must have been
exhausted at this stage, ran to a place between the two sides.
By force of his personality and the respect the people had both
for the man and his office he managed to persuade them to lay
down their arms. This was an incredible achievement on the

part of the priest. The weapons were gathered by trusted men and left in some houses. While Fr Conefry was dealing with this, fresh contingents of men were arriving from all directions. The priest climbed onto the wall surrounding the schoolhouse and delivered a similar speech to the one that had succeeded in disarming the main crowd. He was once more successful. The new arrivals' weapons were deposited in the schoolhouse.

The magistrate in charge, Captain Rogers, called out several times to Fr Conefry, 'Oh! Reverend Sir advise your people, or there will be bloodshed.' While this was going on the priest was walking through the crowds preaching peace and disarming those who still had weapons.

Meanwhile, both forces were edging out of the village towards the first house where a process was to be served. The five hundred police fixed bayonets and charged up the meadow towards the house in question. When they arrived at the building, they were shocked to see that every inch of the area around the house and surrounding fields was full of angry men and women. The men pressed their backs to the walls of the house and stood packed together, many ranks deep, an impenetrable barrier. They were shouting abuse at the advancing police.

The RM read the Riot Act three times and then it was discovered that in fact the house was empty. The fire had been quenched early in the morning and the people had left the house untenanted. No process could be served. It was soon learned that all the other houses had similarly been vacated, so it was not possible to serve process on any of them.

Having failed in his task, the process server was brought back to Drumlish with his military escort. When they got back to the village, a new danger presented itself. The crowd felt that the carboys or 'jarveys' who had brought the police had let their fellow countrymen down and deserved to be taught a lesson. Skilled stone throwers were dispatched to the different roads leading from Drumlish.

Fr Conefry heard what was going on and with the skill of a general he organised some of the most influential and peaceable men to go to the different places where the stone throwers were gathered. Fr Conefry himself took charge of the road leading to Longford, which was the most dangerous position. The first of the jarveys was stoned as they were on the road away from the village. They quickly realised that safe passage was impossible and made a hasty retreat back to Drumlish.

Fearing for the safety of the jarveys and their police passengers, Fr Conefry went to the officer in command and said that if the jarveys and cars went out of Drumlish in small numbers there would be slaughter. The commander agreed and Fr Conefry took hold of the bridle of the horse pulling the first car and led the whole convoy out of the village unmolested. One unfortunate jarvey from Granard was beaten to death on his return home. This ended the second day of the war.

That night riders were out throughout the night in the surrounding towns, villages and townlands getting reinforcements for the tenants. By morning of the third day there were fifteen thousand gathered in Drumlish. They had travelled from about a fifteen-mile radius of the town through snow that was six inches deep in places.

About eleven o'clock in the morning the dragoons, with their gleaming helmets and flashing swords, were seen approaching Drumlish once more. They were followed on foot by the five hundred police, who had to walk as none of the jarveys were willing to risk their lives a second time. Captain Rogers RM, who was in overall command, remarked to a colleague that 'all he had seen of Lord Granard's property was not worth the shedding of a single drop of blood'. This reflected the poor quality of the land from which the tenants were trying to make a living, pay their rents and feed their families. It was the moderation of Captain Rogers and the efforts of Fr Conefry that prevented wholesale bloodshed at this time.

Throughout the third day the troops, police and their fifteen thousand opponents marched, and counter-marched, each trying to outmanoeuvre the other. The net result was that although tensions were high throughout the day, not a single process was served. As the police and troops left Drumlish without any success they announced that they would return the following day with even larger reinforcements. Before the troops left for Longford their commander acknowledged the work that Fr Conefry had done and the influence he had on the people. He also suggested that Fr Conefry should go to Lord Granard in Castle Forbes and use his power of influence and persuasion on His Lordship to get him to abandon his attempts to serve eviction processes.

Fr Conefry did go to Lord Granard that evening and while he was received respectfully, the reception was cold. His Lordship was not in very conciliatory form. He said, 'I believe that Parnell and Dr Croke are at the bottom of all this.' On the morning of the fourth day the ranks of tenants and their supporters had grown even greater than the fifteen thousand that had been present on day three. Neither the dragoons nor police arrived in Drumlish that day. It seemed to the people that they had been victorious. They began to celebrate. Fr Conefry was again to the fore in getting all the public houses to remain closed and so prevent the celebrations getting out of hand.

There was a period of quiet through January and into February. One day in February without warning two companies of cavalry, three companies of infantry, an artillery piece and ambulance wagon as well as a large force of police arrived into the area. This was a force designed to strike terror into the people and to be too strong to be resisted. A petty sessions court was held in Drumlish. Eighty-five men who had been identified as having been the most prominent leaders of the 'rioters' were sent to Mullingar jail.

Sometime later in the year the process server was back in Drumlish with an overwhelming force of troops to make resistance impossible. Over the coming year no fewer than three hundred families were evicted from within a three-mile radius of Drumlish. During 1883 Fr Conefry had the care and settlement of these families on his hands, a task he worked at with his usual energy and influence. In 1884 with the passing of the Arrears Act the tenants were able to be reinstated in their humble homes.

Issues of rent, leases, tenure and land purchase continued in this and other areas into the 1890s. On 16 April 1892 in the Courthouse in Longford, Judge Curran heard a case concerning the tenants of the estate of Lord Granard. The people were represented yet again by Fr Conefry and the outcome was that tenants were able to purchase their homes.

The unnamed author of a work titled *The Land War in Drumlish in 1881* paid a tribute to the sterling work of the parish priest. 'Father Conefry fought the battle of his parishioners with vigour and determination, and it is a consolation to him to find that while he is the hero of one hundred battles for the poor and oppressed, he had won everyone. The example of himself and his people on the historic plains of Drumlish and Ballinamuck shows what can be accomplished by the union of priests and people.'

REFERENCES

The Land War in Drumlish in 1881, pp.1–59, Anon, James Duffy & Co Lth, 1892.

'Memories of the Land War in Drumlish', *Fireside Tales*, p.10, Jude Flynn, 2012.

'The Drumlish Land War and the Irish World', pp.39–42, Prof. Maureen Murphy, *Teathbha*, 2006.

Drumlish Land War Centenary Commemorative Booklet, 1981.

27

THE MAID OF MOYNE

The Harp & Crown was a book of poetry published and printed by the Belfast Newsletter in 1896. Its author and compiler was Joseph A. Latimer. Joe was born on 9 April 1867 in Ballybofey, Co. Donegal. When he was 19, he joined the Royal Irish Constabulary (RIC). While a serving RIC Officer, he developed his interests in both music and poetry and began to publish them from 1887 onwards. 'The Maid of Moyne' is taken from The Harp & Crown.

When the sun is softly setting
O'er Legganommer hills,
And sweet entrancing vespers
The mavis gently trills,
I take my way by Lough Naback,
In ardent haste to join
The fairest maid in all Dromard,
The sweetest girl in Moyne.
You may sing of Cavan County
Where beauteous maids are rife,
And none meet with refusal
Who seek there for a wife;
And you may travel through the land
From Slaney to the Boyne,
And never meet one so fair
As she, the pride of Moyne.

There's some who look to money
When they seek a maiden's hand,
And love is but a trifle

If it brings a spot of land;
But give to me my colleen
Without a single coin,
And I'd marry her tomorrow,
The sweetest girl in Moyne.

There are bright eyes in the Crannagh
As are found anywhere,
They flash forth witching glances
On me at Arvagh Fair;
But they stir up no emotion,
My heart's dictates enjoin
Faithful and deep devotion
To the sweetest girl in Moyne.

The sun, indeed, shall cease to shine
And darkness swallow day,
Ere I prove false unto my heart,
Or from its idol stray,
And would my wish were granted now,
From time I'd soon purloin
The months that shall elapse until
I wed the pride of Moyne.

REFERENCES

The Harp & Crown, Joseph A. Latimer, Belfast Newsletter Office, 1896.

From the Well of St Patrick, James P. MacNerney, St Mel's Diocesan Trust and Dromard History Group, 2000.

28

FOURPENCE OR THE BLESSING OF GOD

This story was told by a man called Fallon. He was born and reared in Newtowncashel and was a postman in the Drumlish area for thirty-nine years. At the time of telling he was living in Barragh-Beg, Drumlish. He happened to be on his céilí and came into the home of Francis Clarke in Barragh-More. James Delaney, the folklore collector, happened to be there at the time.

There were two men and one of them had four pence and the other had nothing. However, the man who had nothing said he 'had the blessing of God'. A discussion developed between the two men as to who was the better off. The man with fourpence said he was better off as he had money. The other man said he was the better off as he had the blessing of God. As the discussion became more heated it soon turned into an argument. It's hard to define when a discussion becomes an argument but when it has, it is quite clear that a change has taken place.

'What will you bet?' asked the man with the money.

'I'll bet my eyes,' said the other. 'I have nothing else to bet.'

As they walked along the road discussing or arguing, they asked the first man they met to settle the bet for them. The man with the money said to the stranger, 'I have fourpence and this man has the grace of God. Which of us is the better off?'

'You are,' said the stranger. So, the man with the money took the sight out of one eye of the other man, the man with the blessing of God.

'Do you continue to bet now?' demanded the money man.

'I will,' said the now one-eyed man with the blessing. 'I'll bet my other eye.'

Sure enough, the next man they met was asked the same question to settle the bet and he gave the same answer that the money man was better off. The man with fourpence took the sight out of his friend's other eye.

The money man led the now blind man further on along the road until they came to an old vacant house. For some reason best known to himself, he put the blind man in under a barrel. The old, almost derelict, house was home to many wild cats. As cats do in these stories, they came in and began to gossip. One of the cats told the story of the man who had lost the sight of both eyes.

Cats being curious creatures, one of them asked if there was anything that would restore the man's sight. Another cat said that there was a well not far away near a bunch of rushes and that the water from this well would cure anything.

Around this same time there was a girl nearby who was very sick. Nobody had been able to cure her, but the cats said the water from the same well would cure her without fail. The girl had a kitten that she would hold in her lap but one day the kitten scratched her. In reply the girl threw the kitten to the floor. In anger the kitten put three 'ribs' of its own hair into the girl's tea and this is what had made her sick in the first instance. There were now three kittens inside the girl.

The blind man heard and understood all this cat chat. He groped his way to the well that the cats had identified. He got some of the well water, rubbed it on to his eyes and, lo and behold, his sight was restored. He found a small empty bottle, which he filled with the well water and made his way to the girl's home.

When he arrived, the girl's father asked him his business and he replied that he had come to cure the daughter. 'And how could you cure her?' demanded the father. 'You're no doctor and every doctor in the country has already tried and failed. What could you do?'

'You better let me as far as her anyway,' he said, 'and if I do no good, I can do no harm.'

So, the father let him see the girl, although he was still very wary of this stranger. The man took the bottle of well water and gave it to the girl. He told her to take a sip. She did and a kitten spewed from her mouth. The girl's father was shocked, amazed and terrified all in the same instant. The man told the girl to take a second sip, which she did, and a second kitten came out her mouth. This was repeated a third time, producing a third kitten. Finally, the man told the girl to take another mouthful of the water to wash it out. This she did and was as right as rain; fully restored to health.

The girl's father was overjoyed. He asked the man where he lived and when he heard that he was living under a barrel at a deserted house he insisted that he stay with the girl's family. This he did and a strong friendship developed between the man and the girl. Eventually the father offered the girl in marriage and built them a house of their own on land close to his own. The young couple married and settled down to a simple but happy life together.

One day long after, a man came to their house and he was in a wretched condition. He was dressed in rags, was dirty and looked as if he hadn't eaten in days. Through the dirt the husband realised that the wretch before him was his old friend, the man who had fourpence. They took him in, cleaned him up and told him he could stay as long as he wanted.

When the man who had had fourpence looked around and saw how well his friend who originally had only the blessing of God was settled he was humbled. He looked into the eyes of his friend, apologised for being so foolish as to think that money was better than the blessing of God and vowed that he had learned his lesson.

They all lived long and well after that, secure in the knowledge that they now all had the grace of God protecting them.

Reference

NFC, 1457; 620–623, Fallon (in Francis Clarke's [82] home), Barragh-Beg, Drumlish, Co. Longford. Jim Delaney 1942.

29

JACK THE THIEF

The bones of this story come from Mr Liam Caddow, who heard it originally from his grandfather. Mr Caddow was of advanced years when this version was documented in 1942. This means that this story was in circulation during the middle years of the nineteenth century, during or after the Famine years.

In the area around Newtownforbes there lived a gentleman and his wife, a substantial landowner who, as well as having plenty of land, was not short of cash. Just because he was rich didn't mean that he threw his money around. He had some workmen working for him at a wage of three shillings per week. One day, the gentleman said to one of his workers, 'Paddy, it can't be easy for you to live on what I'm paying you even though I'm paying the top rate. Now to make things a bit easier for your family, bring up that son of yours Jack to the mansion and I'll pay him a shilling to clean the knives in the kitchen and other jobs around the house.'

The following day, Paddy brought Jack up to the house and introduced him to Her Ladyship. The lady of the house gave him a whole range of small jobs to do. The jobs were not difficult, and they added a most welcome shilling a week to the family income. After a few weeks the housekeeper began to notice that things were going missing. She set a trap and caught the young boy red-handed. The master of the house was furious, especially as he had only been trying to help Paddy's family. 'The best thing you can do with that lad,' said the irate gentleman to Paddy, 'is apprentice him to a thief, at least he's shown an aptitude for that.'

The father set out with the boy the following day. They hadn't gone very far along the road until they came upon two rough-looking characters on horseback.

'Where are you going with that young lad?' demanded one of the riders.

'I'm going to bind him to a thief so he can at least learn that trade.'

'Put him up here behind me,' said the horseman. 'We'll give him his trade for sure.'

The two thieves and their new apprentice were prowling around a wide district in search of opportunities. One day they came to a certain town in the county and went into a prosperous-looking shop. One of the thieves said to the shopkeeper that they had come from another town nearby where a shopkeeper had just been robbed.

'I have no fear of robbers,' said the shopkeeper, 'I have my money well-hidden where nobody could find it.'

'Nothing is impossible to find,' taunted one of the robbers. The poor shopkeeper, of course, was totally unaware of the occupation of his 'customers'. The shopkeeper's ego got the better of his common sense and he brought the three of them in behind the counter, pulled up a secret trapdoor and showed them where he kept his money.

'No robber would ever find that,' he said confidently and proudly. The two thieves and the boy nodded and agreed with the shopkeeper that indeed he wouldn't be fooled by anyone.

That night they got up on the roof of the shop and lowered the boy down the chimney in a bucket. The boy went to the secret hole in the floor and filled the bucket with gold sovereigns and the like. He brought the bucket to the chimney and the robbers hauled it up. They lowered a second bucket, which once more the boy filled with money. The third time they were to pull the boy back up the chimney in the bucket. However, this time the boy filled the bucket with large stones and called to be hoisted. The thieves pulled the bucket halfway up the chimney before letting it fall to the hearth. This is what the lad had expected them to do. Now they had the money they had no need of the boy and wanted to kill him.

The boy was now in a dangerous situation. He was trapped in the shop and the crash of the bucket of rocks must surely have woken the shopkeeper. The shopkeeper dealt in animal hides, so the boy got a cow's skin and quickly wrapped it around himself. He grabbed two cow's horns and held them to the top of his hide. He had just finished when the shopkeeper, resplendent in his nightshirt and two knobbly knees, appeared carrying a small candle. From the top of the stairs he called down, 'Who's there?'

'The Devil's Father is here,' answered Jack in a ghoulish voice, 'and if you don't let me out, I'll burst out through these walls.'

The terrified shopkeeper blew out the candle and scurried back to the safety of his bed.

Jack left the town looking for the two robbers who would have done for him. A couple of miles outside the town he saw a light a little distance off. It was an old abandoned house with two familiar horses tied up outside. The thieves must be inside. Jack approached and through the old kitchen window he saw the two robbers divide the sovereigns into two piles. He still had the cow's hide and horns. In order to scare the robbers, he once more wrapped himself in the hide and held the horns to his head. Without warning he smashed the window, poked his horned head through and let out an unmerciful roar. 'It's the Devil,' cried one of the thieves. They ran from the house, grabbed the two horses and fled as fast as the two old nags could run, never stopping to take the money with them.

Jack took the two buckets of gold and in two days he had returned home. His father and mother were amazed at how successful he was at his new trade. While staying inside his home, Jack gave his father and mother money to buy new clothes and good provisions. Even though he stayed out of sight, it wasn't long before the master in the big house learned of Jack's successful return.

'Paddy is your son home?' the landlord demanded when next he saw the father. Jack's father said that indeed he was home. This shocked the gentleman because Jack was sure to be a thief by this time. His only hope would be to have Jack shot. Together with his wife, the gentleman hatched his plan.

The next day the landlord, who was also the Resident Magistrate, went to Paddy working in the fields and said to him, 'The best horse I have is in the stables. There will be a man on him with a pistol and another man standing at the stable door also with a pistol. Your son Jack the Thief will have to either steal the horse or I'll have him shot for his crimes in the morning.'

Jack's father turned to the RM and said, 'You might as well go down to my house and shoot him now,' because no man could succeed at what had been suggested.

Depressed, the father went home and told Jack of the desperate situation he was in. 'Oh,' said Jack, 'anyone could do that.'

Jack went into town and bought three bottles of whiskey. At about eleven o'clock that night Jack rambled quietly up towards the stables. At the side of the stable was a large mound of manure and lying on top of the manure was a large sow. Jack lay alongside the sow and began to feed her some of the whiskey. The two men inside the stable guarding the horse heard the grunts of the sow. 'Do you think the sow is going to have bonaves (piglets)?' one man said to the other. 'If anything happens to that sow the gentleman will have our guts for garters. Jack can't steal this horse with me sitting on him and a loaded pistol in my hand. Go out and check the sow and I'll blow Jack's brains out if he as much as looks into this stable.'

The guard who was standing at the door went out to the sow, who appeared to be terribly drunk for a pig. Moreover, there was a fellow fast asleep beside the pig and he also appeared to be drunk, at least from the smell of whiskey rising off him. It was then that the man saw the whiskey bottle sticking out of his pocket. He shook the body, not a stir. He took the whiskey from the man's pocket and returned inside the stable. He held up the bottle of whiskey and told his companion that there was a man asleep outside who was crooked drunk.

'It's a cold night and we'll be glad of a little inside warming.' He handed the bottle up to the guard sitting on the horse. Between them it didn't take long before the five-naggin bottle was empty and the two men were in high form.

They decided the guard on the door should go out and search the drunk for more whiskey. Eventually he found two more bottles on the body one full, one half full. These he brought inside. 'Get down off that horse for God's sake,' he said on his return. 'How could he get in with the two of us here? Wouldn't we blow his brains out before he could get near the horse.'

So, the pair settled down for a good drinking session. Before long one fell asleep, followed not long after by the other guard. When Jack was sure both men were fast asleep, he quietly walked into the stable, took the horse, brought it home and tied its reins to a bush.

About dawn the old gentleman came out of the mansion and down to the stables just as one of the guards awoke and rubbed his eyes. 'Where's my horse,' shouted the master, promptly sacking the two 'guards'.

The master returned to the mansion and told his wife what had happened. 'You can't trust anybody. We'll have to deal with that thief ourselves.'

Knowing full well that Jack was responsible for the missing horse, they went into consultation and came up with their plan.

When Jack's father, Paddy, came to work a little later the old gentleman went out to him and said, 'Paddy, go down and tell your son he'll have to take the sheet from under myself and my wife tonight and I'll have the light lighting and a double-barrelled shotgun ready loaded.'

'You might as well go and shoot him now,' said Jack's father, 'for nobody could do what you're challenging.'

'Just go and tell him,' the master said, ending any further discussion on the matter.

Paddy went home downheartedly and told Jack. 'That's nothing,' smiled Jack. 'Sure wouldn't anyone be able to do that.'

Jack was easily recognisable in the area because of the grey suit he had worn for a long, long time. Now it so happened that only a few days earlier a young lad of about the same age and build as Jack had died tragically and was buried. As soon as it was dark, Jack exhumed the body and dressed it in his distinctively dirty grey suit. He then managed to carry the corpse to the manor and up to the top of the roof. Putting a rope under the arms of the dead body, he began to lower it down the chimney. The gentleman and his wife heard the noise in the chimney. As the legs appeared at the bottom of the chimney, he grabbed the shotgun and waited until the torso was in view. Bang, bang! He fired both barrels, blasting a hole in the body that you could put your fist through.

'Oh, put out the light,' said Her Ladyship. 'I can't look at something so horrific.'

Jack quickly withdrew the rope and let the corpse slump into the hearth.

'You've killed him, what are you going to do with the body now?' asked the wife timidly.

'I'm going to dig a hole in the garden right now and bury him in it,' was the reply.

The gentleman dragged the body to the garden, got a spade and began to dig a grave. As soon as Jack saw the man engaged in the digging, he slipped into the house, up and into the bedroom, where Her Ladyship was. Mimicking the gentleman's voice, he said, 'It's freezing outside I think I need a roll and a cuddle before I do any more.'

In the pitch darkness Her Ladyship didn't realise it was Jack. He tickled her and she jumped around the bed. As they frolicked in the bed, Jack worked the bedsheet till he got it off the bed. When he had succeeded, he told her that he had best finish burying Jack.

He had hardly left when the gentleman returned to his bed chamber. 'You weren't long,' said the wife.

'Long, me granny!' said the gentleman. 'I've been out there ever since, and I'm frozen with the cold.'

'But,' she said to him, 'you weren't gone long the first time when you came back for a heat and a cuddle in the bed.'

'I never came back,' he said, 'and if anyone came it must have been that thief of the world.'

They lit the light and sure enough the sheet was gone.

'He's done it again,' said the old gentleman. His wife was mortified when she remembered rolling in the bed with Jack, whom she had thought was her husband. She said that she had been scandalised, and further that she wouldn't stay another day or night in that house.

The master realised that his suggestion that Jack should be apprenticed to a thief had backfired on him completely. He was forced to acknowledge that Jack was the 'winner'. As his wife wouldn't live in the manor again, the gentleman gave the house to Paddy, his wife and family including Jack the Thief. For all I know they could be living there still.

REFERENCE

NFC 1429, 45–54, Liam Caddow, Jim Delaney, 1942.

30

THE CANNON CHAINS
AND GUNNER MAGEE

The Battle of Ballinamuck was a seminal moment, not just in the history of the 1798 Rebellion but in the history and folk memory of the people of Co. Longford. The battle marked the end of the French expeditionary force under General Humbert, who surrendered himself and his troops after the battle. It also saw the slaughter of many Irish 'croppies', who were either summarily executed or simply pursued and cut down as they tried to escape the battle area. It is beyond the scope here to give a full account of the battle and the events leading to it but rather to give account of two episodes that have lived for over two hundred years in the folklore of Co. Longford.

The 1798 Rebellion began in May of that year and fighting quickly spread to many parts of the country. On 22 August, a force of about a thousand French troops, under the command of General Humbert, landed at Killala Bay, Co. Mayo. The French were quickly joined by the rebel Irish force. They had great initial success by defeating the British at Castlebar. Indeed, so quick was the British retreat that it became known as the 'Castlebar Races'.

The French and Irish rebels planned initially to make for Ulster but, hearing incorrectly that the midlands were under rebel control, left Castlebar on 4 September and headed from Mayo, through Sligo, into Leitrim and towards Granard. This was a gruelling forced march. The French–Irish force were being pursued by British troops led by General Lake, who were following in their rear with a force of fifteen thousand men. Lord Cornwallis, meantime, was leading a large force north-westwards to intercept them. General Humbert was aware of the danger of being encircled by two large enemy forces. He therefore decided to make a stand and give battle from a defensive position of his choosing.

By 7 September the Franco–Irish force had reached Cloone, Co. Leitrim. Here they rested for the night.

> At Cloone in fair Leitrim they rested,
> For two days then Dublin they struck,
> And mounted on the eight of September
> The hillsides of Ballinamuck.

The French officers rested at the home of William West, a rich Protestant farmer. In the folklore it is said that Mr West showed great hospitality and showered his guests with food and drink of the best. They overdid it on the drink and as a result overslept next morning, the morning of 8 September, the fateful day of the Battle of Ballinamuck.

In their haste upon waking, they were unable to find the chains that were needed to haul the artillery pieces and limbers that would be so needed in any upcoming battle. Vital hours were lost searching for the chains while all the time they knew that the advancing British to their rear were closing. The conclusion was that the chains had been stolen during the night.

There are many theories and stories about what happened to the 'stolen chains'. One finger of suspicion pointed to West who, it was said, had stolen the vital chains and thrown them down a deep well. Other members of the West family and their servants also came under suspicion. A more innocent explanation is that, knowing the importance of the chains to the artillery, the chains had been brought into the house when the French arrived on the evening of the seventh and covered with hay.

In the darkness and panic of their oversleeping nobody could find the chains, nor remember where they had been hidden. It was also said that after the troops left Mr West eventually found the chains and dropped them into a well because he was afraid. He would be accused of their theft if they had been discovered on his property. Another suspected of their stealing was 'a wretch' called Neary, who had originally been employed by Mr West.

Whatever the cause, the fact was that the chains were gone, and valuable time had been lost. Time that might have allowed the French and Irish to reach and defend from the town of Granard, a naturally excellent defensive position. Necessity is the mother of invention, and the guns were manhandled with ropes. Progress, however, was slow, and the pursuing British were getting ever nearer. In order to maintain speed some of the artillery pieces, their limbers and ammunition were dumped into Keeldra Lough. The result was that only two cannon were in the passion of the Franco-Irish troops as they approached Ballinamuck.

General Humbert knew that he could not reach Granard and so decided to halt and give battle to the English, who were approaching on two fronts. The location he chose was Ballinamuck. He drew up his troops on the high ground around the village. The main force of pike men was placed on Shanmullagh Hill to the north-east. The rest of his troops, including the two cannon under the charge of Gunner Casey and Gunner Magee, were positioned on high ground, southeast of the village, commanding the road leading from Cloone from where General Lake's force could be expected. The guns were deployed at the Black Fort near Gaigue.

The two field pieces they had were six-pounders with smooth bore and were loaded from the front or muzzle. This weapon was greatly liked by Napoleon, who himself had originally been an artillery officer.

Gunner James Magee had originally been a member of the Royal Longford Militia (a British force) led by the Earl of

Granard. It is thought that at some stage in his career he had been a member of the Royal Irish Artillery Regiment, where he would have learned his trade as a gunner. It was not uncommon for members of local militias to have been trained in gunnery by the Royal Irish Artillery Regiment.

For reasons that seem to remain unclear, both Gunners Casey and Magee decided to desert the Longford Militia and join the rebels after the Battle of Castlebar. They simply turned their redcoats inside out and became, as would later be seen, a very valuable asset to the rebel cause.

When the battle started at about 8 a.m., the artillery on both sides fired on each other. Eventually a shell, or more rightly, a cannon ball from a British gun smashed Gunner Casey's gun and put it out of action. This increased the morale of the British and they rallied.

Gunner Magee always referred to his six-pounder as 'Aunt Kate'. Aunt Kate spoke loud and clear that day. Tradition has it that a 'chain ball' from Gunner Magee's gun halted the British progress. A chain ball is two cannonballs joined by a length of chain. When the cannon is fired the balls spread out to the length of the chain and fly parallel to the ground. The taut chain could carry off men, horses and heads to great effect.

Magee fired a second 'chain-ball' shot and this hit a British ammunition limber, which exploded. Before long Magee's ammunition was running low and tradition has it that he had all the bits of metal – bolts, pans, stones and anything else at hand – loaded into the muzzle of his cannon and fired. This had the effect of 'canister', effectively turning a cannon into an over-sized shotgun. This also had a significant impact on the British.

Magee was in the process of reloading the cannon when its carriage was hit by an English cannonball, which broke the right wheel and rendered the gun useless. In order that the gun could fire again, several rebels lifted the heavy bronze cannon on to their shoulders and physically aimed it at the enemy. Magee fired the cannon successfully, but the recoil killed those holding it.

By about 9 a.m. the French surrendered their swords and the officers and men were well treated as prisoners of war. The Irish knew there would be no such terms for them. This was especially true for Gunner Magee, who would not only be seen as an enemy but as a traitor. Accounts say that Magee remained at his shattered gun, grabbed a pike and fought the advancing enemies until he was overpowered and taken prisoner. He was given a drumhead court martial, sentenced and hanged.

Many of the other rebels were captured or hunted down as they tried to escape through the fields and bogs around Shanmullagh Hill. Those that were taken prisoner were brought to Jack Griffin's house in Coilte Craobhach. The first to be hanged was General Blake, the Irish Commander, who was hanged from the raised shafts of a two-wheeled cart. Blake was buried in Tubberpatrick graveyard, just off the road to Arva. They then began hanging the rest of the prisoners. There were so many of them that the British troops were getting exhausted with the task. They decided to pick victims by a lottery. If a man drew 'life' he was released but anyone who drew 'death' was hanged.

The Irish that were killed that day were all buried in pits by the roadside. The English dead weren't buried at the battlefield but were loaded on to carts and taken away.

Ballinamuck and the defeat of the French and Irish force effectively marked the end of the Rebellion. The Rebellion had lasted from 23 May until 8 September 1798.

While Saint Barbara is the patron saint of gunners in every country, the Artillery Corps of the Irish Army is the only arm of the Defence Forces to have an historical figurehead. That figurehead is Gunner James Magee for the enduring values of 'respect, loyalty, selflessness, physical courage, moral courage and integrity'.

References

'Traditions of 1798: The Battle of Ballinamuck', pp.393–395, Pádraig Mac Gréine, *Bealoideas*, Vol. 4, No. 4, 1934.

https://www.militaryheritage.ie/wp-content/uploads/2018/11/Gunner-Magee-Defender-of-Arty-Corps-Values.pdf, Brigadier-General Paul A. Pakenham (retd), Sept 2018.

The Battle of Ballinamuck, pp.1–7, James O'Neill, National Graves Association.

Killoe, History of a Longford Parish, pp.125–137, Rev. Owen Devaney.

Undaunted by Gibbet and Yeos, pp.2–43, Des Guckian, 1998.

NFC S225, 144–5, NFC S758: 438–441, NFC 1858: pp.42–42.

31

THE KING CONGAL
OF GRANARD

There are many stories told about the days long ago when the O'Farrells ruled in Granard. Granard was their royal base and a stronghold few would dare attack.

King Congal of the O'Farrell clan was married to the most beautiful lady in the whole of Leinster. Their marriage was a love match and not an arranged political marriage as was common with so many of the marriages among the clans. It was love at first sight for Congal and his beautiful young bride.

She was due to give birth to their first child following an uneventful pregnancy, when she unexpectedly died in childbirth. Congal was stunned. The wife that he loved was gone. He couldn't come to terms with the suddenness of her death. He suspected that his chief Druid had played some role in her death. The more he thought about it, the more he convinced himself that the Druid had used his special powers and rites to bring about her death. The Druid was to blame. Guilty!

He was so angry at what he believed the Druid had done that he ordered his execution to take place exactly one year from the date and time his wife had passed away. Knowing he was going to be executed would add mental turmoil to the Druid, which was all he deserved.

The Druid claimed he was innocent. He had no reason to want Congal's wife dead. In fact, he had been supportive of her from the very day she arrived in Granard. Congal would hear none of it. Execution in exactly one year was the sentence.

Congal became a recluse in his grief. He locked himself away in his chambers and refused to see anyone nor let anyone see him. This caused great concern among Congal's courtiers. Every clan needed a chieftain. It was like a body; a clan without a king was like a body without a head. They tried everything possible to get Congal to emerge from his chambers and resume his role. Nothing worked.

Time rolled on and the first anniversary of Congal's wife's death was fast approaching. Anxiety was high for the chief Druid and his family. They hoped that the passage of time might have mellowed Congal's grief and that his life would be spared after all. Perhaps this was just wishful thinking and the day of reckoning loomed. As the day drew nearer, the Druid's eldest daughter convinced her father to let her try to intercede on his behalf.

The Druid's daughter disguised herself as a servant and stayed close to Congal's quarters. She was hoping against hope that she would get an opportunity to meet the king and to plead for her father's life. She waited and waited until finally an opportunity presented itself. The king called for a cup of pure spring water. The girl quickly got it and brought it to him. As soon as she was in his presence she fell to the floor and begged forgiveness for her father on the grounds that he was innocent of the charges Congal had made against him.

The king was struck by her beauty and the way she pleaded for her father's life. Finally, Congal told her that if she attended him every day for twelve days, he would have had time to consider her request and would give her an answer.

Each day at the same time she brought the same drink to the King. As the days past she sensed a relaxing of his stern manner. If truth be known, as the days passed Congal looked forward more and more to her daily visit. On the twelfth day he granted the chief Druid a full pardon and restored him to his high office within the O'Farrell clan.

Congal also asked the girl to take the place of his wife who had died a year earlier. This request was against the law of the land as the king could not marry beneath his station without the express permission of his people. The influential members of the clan were horrified at Congal's request to marry the Druid's daughter and immediately refused. Congal begged and pleaded with his people in a very unkinglike manner. Their permission was not forthcoming.

Congal was torn between his duty to his clan and the new love he had found for the Druid's daughter. For months he agonised over what he should do. Should he continue as king, alone without a new queen? Should he abandon the throne and follow his heart?

As time passed it became clearer and clearer to Congal what he must do. He called the council of the clan and announced he was going to abdicate the throne. This he did but not before first appointing his successor.

The king, now a commoner, asked the Druid's permission to marry his daughter. The Druid was not a vindictive man. He gave his blessing and Congal and his daughter were married. They went on to live a full and happy life together.

REFERENCE

Historical Notes and Stories of the County Longford, pp.93–94, J.P. Farrell, Dollard, Dublin, 1886.

32

A Raking Pot of Tea

Ireland has long been one of the highest per capita consumers of tea in the world. Tea in Ireland is seen as the universal panacea. A cup of tea will cheer you up if you are having a bad day, and can be used to relax if you are having a good one. Tea will warm you if you are cold and cool you if you are hot. However, the tea that occupies so much shelf space in our supermarkets today, has had, to say the least, a chequered past.

Tea drinking in Ireland, originally as in England, was the preserve of the upper classes. Tea was so expensive that it was kept in a locked box with the head butler being in sole charge of the key. During the eighteenth century the lower classes began to want a better quality of life and they too began to drink tea.

Tea drinking in Ireland was not common among the poorest people until about 1830. Tea consumption continued to increase, and many reformers started writing pamphlets warning of the dangers of tea drinking, especially among women. One of the principal worries of these reformers was that poorer women could not afford tea and that their meagre income could not cover tea as well as the essential food that was needed, especially by their children and their husbands who had to do heavy physical labour to survive.

Maria Edgeworth from Edgeworthstown was one of the reformers. In her novel *Castle Rackrent* she refers to a 'raking pot of tea'. In the glossary she explains what this means:

> The time when the festive ceremony begins varies according to circumstances; but it is never earlier that twelve o'clock at night – the

joys of a raking pot of tea depending on it being made in secret, and at an unseasonable hour. After a ball, when the more discreet part of the company has departed to rest, a few chosen females … call the favourite maid, who alone is admitted, bid her put down the kettle, lock the door, and amid as much giggling and scrambling as possible they get around a tea-table, on which all manner of things are huddled together.

This was seen as decadent and contributing to a type of ritualism that was undesirable. While this might be acceptable in higher society, it would be the ruination of the lower classes if women began wasting their time drinking tea and ignoring the duties they were expected to perform.

When tea was first introduced to Ireland it was not readily available in shops but was distributed around the country by tea sellers known as 'tea men'. One account was given by Joy Moorhead from Edgeworthstown: 'Long years ago before tea was to be got so handy in shops as it is today, men used to drive around in big high cars selling it. They stopped at every house and forced the people to buy some whether they were willing or not.

'They used to walk into everyone's house and leave them a certain amount of tea and next week they would call for the price of it. Very often the poor people could not afford to buy any but all the same the supply was left with them as if they were able to pay for it.'

Many plans were got up to trick the 'tea men' or 'tae man' as they were known. One old man named Patrick Gilchriest played a great trick on one. This tae man left him one pound of tea and said he would call in a week for the price of it or if not the pound of tea returned. Patrick emptied the bag of tea and filled it with turf mould. When the tea man called, he gave him the bag saying that he had no money to pay for it and did not keep it. The tea man left with the turf mould.

Another old man named Myles Reily from Cranly who was left a big supply of tea, used it but had no money to pay in return. Reily and some friends from Cranly were chatting one night by the fireside about how they would best trick the tae man. They thought of a plan and they made up a bed underneath his kitchen window and put the old man in the bed dressed as one who was dead. They placed a table with seven lighted candles alongside the bed.

When the tea man arrived, he asked for the boss of the house and one of the boys said, 'Oh, he is after dying poor soul. Will you forgive him his debts to you?' The tea man said he would, knelt by the bedside and showed signs of sorrow. The tea man left and never came back to Myles Reily's house again.

Perhaps the most common folk tale about tea regarded people's initial lack of knowledge about how tea should be made. One such tale from Co. Longford was told by Peter McDermott, who was born in 1890 and died in 1982 in Moydow. He had heard this story from his grandmother, who had died when Peter was only ten years old.

Peter's father was born in 1846 and tea was unknown in their household at that time. Their breakfast was oaten porridge or 'stirabout' with buttermilk, to which some ordinary milk was added. Their main meal of the day was usually bacon, potatoes and whatever vegetables were in season. The final evening meal was more stirabout taken after the day's work had been completed.

Because Friday was a day of abstinence, their dinner was oaten bread, potatoes, butter and two blue duck eggs. Butter was only ever used for Friday's dinner. Tea had become common in Peter's young years but was only taken in the morning and evening and never after dinner.

Peter recounted a story his grandmother used to tell about herself. She had been born Kitty McGarry in 1817 and when she was sixteen she was attending a 'station' in her aunt's house in Clough. A 'station' was a very special occasion. The priest would come and celebrate Mass in the house and all the neighbours would attend. It was therefore only natural that you would want your place to look right or your neighbours would be talking about you. If your home was selected for a station it would be the highlight of the year. Every building and wall would be whitewashed, and all outstanding repairs to the buildings were carried out so the property would be looking its best.

The table in the 'good room' would be set out with the best cutlery and plates because it was the custom to serve the priest his breakfast when Mass was over. The head of the house and selected guests would join the priest for this mini 'feast'. There was a china cup and saucer and plate for the priest. There were large cups for the men who would be at the breakfast. These were over half-pint capacity. There was also oaten bread and wholemeal bread, eggs and butter. There were also two duck eggs for the priest.

When the aunt heard she was having a station she naturally wanted to impress the priest with her culinary skills. She sent into Mr Little's shop in Kenagh for a quarter pound of tea, a white loaf and two pounds of sugar.

Peter's grandmother, then a sixteen-year-old, was told to make the tea. She was given the instruction 'put it in a burner and give it a thundering boil'. This she did and when she considered that a thundering boil had been completed, she threw out the water, put the tea leaves on a plate, sprinkled them with sugar and brought them to the priest in the good room.

'What's that, Kitty?' asked the priest.

'That's tea, Father.'

'And Kitty what did you do with the water?' asked the priest.

'I thrun (threw) it out,' she said.

The priest asked if there was more tea in the kitchen, which Kitty said there was. The priest went to the kitchen and made proper tea for himself and each man at the breakfast.

There was a man named Robin Harte, who was a thatcher at the breakfast. Later, as a very old man he used to call regularly at the McDermott home. Anytime he wanted to annoy Peter's elderly grandmother Robin used to say to her, 'God be with the day ye spoiled me breakfast.'

This always got the desired response from poor old Kitty McDermott.

There were also some Co. Longford riddles about tea:

Question: 'Why is weak tea like a bad picture?'
Answer: 'Because neither is well drawn.'

Mrs John Kenny (56), Formoyle

Question: 'What goes in dry and comes out wet and everybody likes it?'

Answer: 'Tea going into a teapot.'

Mary Fanning, Garrowhill

Question: I have a little unicorn,
She gives milk, but she's no Kerry Cow.
My Grandmother loves her.
All round the bush shoves her,
With a smile of good luck on her brow.
Answer: A teapot

Irene Finnegan, Forgney.

REFERENCES

Tales and Novels' Vols 1 & 2 containing Castle Rackrent, p.48, Maria Edgeworth, Harper & Brothers, New York, 1846.

https://www.britainexpress.com/History/tea-in-britain.htm, David Ross.

Cottage Dialogues Among the Irish Peasantry: With Notes and a Preface by Maria Edgeworth, Mary Leadbeater, London, 1811.

NFCS 0770: 364–365, Joy Moorhead, Main Street, Edgeworthstown, Co. Longford. Mostrim National School, Richard Hyland, 1938.

'Tea for the Priest', *Teathba* Vol. 2, No. 2, Jim Delaney.

https://www.duchas.ie/en/cbes/5009138/4990434/5101265

https://www.duchas.ie/en/cbes/5009158/4992832

https://www.duchas.ie/en/cbes/5009146/4991510/5100998

33

THE LITTLE RED BULL

This folk tale was told by James Martin of Drumbeg, Ballinalee. James was 71 when he told it sometime before 1930. Mr Martin was a stone-mason by trade, described as being an 'intelligent man' who was able to both read and write. Apart from a short time spent in Scotland, he plied his trade in Longford and surrounding counties. As well as a storyteller, he was a fine singer in a traditional style with a wide reper-toire. Like many folk tales, this story begins with a king and a queen.

Long and long ago it was there was a king and queen in Ireland who had one son. The boy was still an infant when his mother, the queen, died suddenly. The poor king was heartbroken, but he was still a young man and after a few years he married another woman and made her queen. As this woman was independently rich it was the status of being queen that she desired. She may have married the king but got a stepson as a 'bonus'. This was a prize she gladly would have done without. To put it simply, she hated the boy. Time passed and she had children of her own. This only served to deepen her hatred of the stepson.

To get the boy out of her sight she persuaded her husband, the king, to send the teenage boy up the mountains to tend the cattle. The youth was lonely on the windswept hillsides and very miser-able at the way his life was turning out. He was frail looking, with a grey pallor and his ribs sticking out like piano keys. There was a little red bull in the herd who noticed him crying. The bull came over to the boy and asked why he was so upset. The boy explained his circumstances; that he was always underfed and made to sleep outside while the rest of his so-called family were inside the castle living the high life.

'Well,' said the Little Red Bull, 'if you unscrew one of my horns you will find all you want to eat there. The spirit of your late mother is in me and I don't want you to be afraid any more. Anytime you need anything just come and tell me.'

The young ex-prince was stunned for not only had the bull spoken but had said the spirit of his mother resided in him. At once his spirits lifted. As instructed, he unscrewed the horn and, how he did not know, inside there was a knife, a tablecloth and all manner of food and drink of the best. When he had fully satisfied his appetite, he returned the tablecloth inside the horn and screwed it back in place on the head of the little red bull. 'I'll come every day and feed you,' said the bull.

The bull was true to its word and every day he would leave the herd and come to the boy and provide all the nourishment he needed. Day by day the boy grew stronger. The colour returned to his cheeks, his chest filled out and he became the picture of ruddy good health. It wasn't long before the queen noticed the change not only in his appearance but in his agility and strength. She questioned all the servants, demanding to know if any of them had been feeding the youth. They all assured her that they had not.

Stronger and stronger the boy became until he was bigger and more robust than any other youth of his age in the whole kingdom. The queen hated seeing him look so well and it only strengthened her hatred of the lad. One day she saw the little red bull walking away from the youth and she began to suspect that there was some connection between the change that had come over her stepson and the bull.

'I feel sick,' she told the king, 'I fear I have a weakness in my blood. If only I ate the heart and liver of that little red bull, I'm sure I'd be restored to full health.'

'Don't be silly woman,' said the king, 'that little red bull is only a runt. If it's heart and liver you need, I'll kill one of the larger bulls and have the organs cooked for you in the kitchen.'

'No,' the queen insisted angrily, it was the organs of the little red bull that she needed.

'Never argue with an angry woman,' thought the king to himself.

Later that night they surrounded the little red bull and tried to catch him. They failed. The bull knew, however, that it was only a matter of time till he was taken and slaughtered. He told the boy that he would try to evade his tormentors for as long as he could and continue feeding the young prince.

At the same time as all this was going on there was a family of giants living in a big castle in the woods. There were four giants and their mother, a giantess. Everybody stayed well away from them. The boy had been warned by his father the king to never let the cattle stray into the woods and on to the giants' land. The boy was so worried at the fate that awaited his little red bull that he became preoccupied and one day the herd strayed into the forest and the land of the giants. The giants milked all the cattle and really enjoyed the beautiful rich creamy milk. That evening the cattle wandered out of the forest just as they had wandered in.

The following day the giants were watching for the cows now that they had a taste for their milk. As the boy was driving the herd, one of the giants made a charge for him. In a flash the little red bull saw the danger and said to the boy, 'Get up on my back and the giant won't catch us. Be sure however that you touch neither a tree nor a branch when we are going through the forest. In the forest there lives a giant bull and if you touch a branch or a tree it will ring out, the giant bull will be alerted, and I'll have to fight it.'

The boy said he would be careful and do as the little red bull said. 'Just in case,' said the bull, the spirit of his late mother, 'if I get killed you must skin me and always keep the skin with you. If ever you are in danger, then just stand on my skin and swear by the heart and liver of the little red bull and you'll prevail over whatever danger you are in.'

This upset the lad because the bull had been so good to him that the thought of anything happening to it didn't bear thinking about. Anyway, the lad jumped on the back of the bull and away they flew from the giant. Faster and faster they went until the giant started to lose ground. The boy looked round and at that very moment failed to see an approaching branch. He struck the branch and the loudest ringing ever heard sounded throughout the whole forest. The ringing was quickly followed by the most terrifying roar of the giant bull.

The red bull told the boy to climb a tree for safety. It then turned to face the charge of the oncoming giant bull. The giant bull was roaring and clawing the ground until the whole forest seemed to shake. The little red bull stood his ground and as the two bulls met the little bull managed to get his horn under the giant bull and rip it open, killing it instantly.

The boy asked the bull if he was all right. The bull said he was but that he would have to fight another bull the next day. He knew that the next bull would be ten times the size of the one just slain. The next day the youth and the little red bull found themselves once more straying into the forest, where yet again they were chased by the giant. The red bull issued the same instructions to his young friend: avoid any contact with branches or trees.

Once more they fled and again outpaced the huge strides of the giant. Unfortunately, the young bull rider brushed against a branch. The forest rang loudly and the terrifying roar of a bull much louder than the previous one could be heard. The boy was again instructed to climb a tree to safety. This bull was a monster. Fearlessly, the little red bull turned to face the onslaught, but he was no match for his new foe. Within seconds the little bull lay dead on the ground. The youth waited up the tree until all was quiet once more with neither sight nor sound of either the giant or the bull.

He got down from the tree, and with tears running down his cheeks, he unscrewed the bull's horn, retrieved the knife it held and skinned the little red bull that had been so good to him. He was so sad at being alone and so absorbed in his thoughts that he paid no heed to the cows as they strayed once more into the forest.

The following day, a giant emerged from the forest and said he would kill the boy for letting the cattle graze on their land. The boy laid down the bull's skin, stood on it, and swore by the heart and liver of the little red bull that he would prevail. The giant lunged in attack and was swiftly killed by the boy. Day after day another giant would emerge from the forest, only for the youth to stand on the skin, utter the oath and kill his aggressor.

This continued until at last there was only one giant remaining. The lad decided to take the fight to the enemy and headed for the giant's castle. When he entered the castle there was a huge old woman giant, the last giant's mother, sitting by the fire.

'What are you doing here?' she demanded. 'When my eldest son returns, he'll eat you for sure because he hates mere mortals as yourself.'

The boy pretended to be frightened, 'Is there any place I can hide?'

'There's no way I can hide you because he'll smell you for sure, but I wouldn't like to see you being eaten so I'll put you here in the giant-sized cupboard behind me.'

The youth was only just inside the cupboard when the giant returned. 'I smell, I smell, I smell a man, and I'll have his blood for me mornin' dram.'

The final giant pulled the door of the cupboard open, but the boy was standing on the red bull's skin and, calling on the bull's heart and liver, easily slew the giant. The giant mother was lamenting the loss of her last son, even though he was one very ugly giant. The boy assured her that he would do her no harm. Before he left the castle, he decided to explore it. He was amazed, in virtually every room there was gold, silver, jewels and all manner of wealth that the giant family had robbed over the years.

He left the castle but returned the following day. This time he inspected the stables, where there were four great horses. The horses needed to be fed because the giants had all been killed and the mother had taken to her bed in sorrow. He fed the horses and admired their strong muscles and great size.

It just so happened, as it so often does in stories, that there was to be a hunt that very day. The boy dressed himself in his best clothes, put gold guards on his arms and let his long gold blond hair out from under his cap. The hair flowed over his shoulders. He went to the hunt, where among the riders were his half-sisters and all the gentry from near and far. Nobody recognised him but all wondered who the fine young man was on the great black horse.

The hunt started but none of the riders were able to keep pace with the hounds. None that is except the gold-haired young man and one beautiful young woman who was not from that district. However large an obstacle the young man set his steed to, the young lady would choose an even more difficult route. Soon they were having a rare old time finding ever harder hurdles to jump in order to keep with the hounds. When the hunt was over, the two riders spoke briefly, then the young man rode off and disappeared before the other hunters caught up with them.

That night the youth, his hair pushed back under his cap, put on his old clothes and returned to his home, where the king, the queen and the half-brothers and sisters lived. He sat and listened as they talked about the hunt and the adventures they had. Everyone wanted to know who was the beautiful young man with the golden hair. He grew tired of their chatter and withdrew to the loft of the barn, the only place he was allowed to sleep. Before he reached the barn, he changed his mind. Why should he sleep in such an uncomfortable place when the giants' mother had such a 'fáilte' (welcome) for him even though he had killed her sons in self-defence?

He returned to the castle in the forest and was indeed welcomed by the mother, who was very lonely now that her sons were gone. She gave him one of the best rooms in the castle and he had the best sleep he'd had for years. He had breakfast, fed the horses and saddled the mount he had ridden at the hunt and rode about the countryside. As he passed a certain nobleman's house some distance from his own area, he saw the young woman who had hunted so well with him.

He stopped to talk with her, and it was love at first or perhaps second sight. He told her to saddle her hunter and he would show her the castle where he now lived. She was amazed at all the gold, silver, jewels that were scattered about. The giant mother could see that they were obviously in love and said that they could have the castle and all that was in it. She told them that this land held nothing for her now and that she was leaving to stay with her sister, a giant in another land.

As they rode back to the young lady's house, the blond-haired youth, our hero, asked her to marry him. She agreed, 'Providing,' she said, 'that my father approves.' The following day the boy approached the father and asked for his daughter's hand. The father was overjoyed and approved unconditionally.

Before long, news of the betrothal spread and when the step-mother heard of his good fortune she flew into a rage, ran to the battlement of her castle and let out a piercing scream. As she screamed, she lost her balance and fell to her death in the moat below. The following day, the young couple brought the young lady's father over to see their fine new castle once owned by the giants. When the girl's father realised it was the giants' castle and that they were all dead he was overjoyed. He had been paying large sums of gold to these giants as protection money, indeed most of the noblemen in the surrounding districts had all been paying tributes to them.

The boy, now a young man with a new bride, went to his father, the king. The king was very remorseful for the way his son had been treated. There was no bitterness in the lad as he knew it was the fault of his late stepmother and not his father.

The lad settled down with his wife and in the fullness of time they were in the middle of their own family. He lived a rich life for many years on the wealth that was in the old giants' castle and neither he nor his family wanted for anything. However, through all those years his greatest treasure and greatest wealth was the skin of the little red bull that he always kept with him. When he was dying, he made his eldest son promise to always take care of the skin and to use its powers wisely. He passed away and to nobody's surprise the little red bull skin lost all its powers and was buried with him so that the son and the spirit of his mother could be together for all time.

REFERENCE

Bealoideas, Vol. 2, No. 3, pp.268–272, 1930.

34

PENNY WISE AND POUND FOOLISH

*The Forbes family have long been associated with Co. Longford, espe-
cially in the parish of Clongesh and the village of Newtownforbes.
The Forbes were known to be a frugal family who were not lavish
with their spending. The 5th Earl of Granard, George Forbes, was
born in April 1740. His first wife died while young and the Earl
remarried Lady Georgina Augusta Berkeley in 1766.*

Lady Georgina was a very kind and generous lady who believed
that 'those who give to the poor lend to the Lord'. This was not
a sentiment shared by her husband, the 5th Earl, who shared the
family reputation for being 'tight' with his money.

One day, Sir George and Lady Georgina were strolling in the
beautiful grounds of their estate at Newtownforbes. It was a
sunny day, all was well in their world and Lady Georgina was in
particularly good humour. As they walked, they were approached
by a poor beggar, whose very appearance appalled Sir George.
The beggar with lifeless eyes was unwashed, dressed in rags and
shoeless. He begged the couple for some alms with which he
could feed himself and his family.

Lady Georgina, being of a giving disposition, smiled at
the poor wretch bowing before her with his dirty hand outstretched. She did not recoil from the odours that rose in waves
from the poor wretch, unlike her husband who held his hand-
kerchief over his mouth and nose. Her Ladyship took out her
purse and took a guinea from it. Without hesitation, she gave
the beggar the coin. The beggar's eyes lit up and for once the

light of hope returned to them. With much touching of his forelock, he backed away from the couple and began to leave the estate, for once a happy man.

When Sir George saw how much she had given the poor wretch he was next to speechless. He admonished his wife for being over-generous and began to lecture her on the need to keep a tight rein on the family's money. He reminded his wife that 'guineas were not so plentiful as to be given away at random'. His wife listened dutifully.

When his lecture had ended, Lady Georgina asked her husband to loan her a half-sovereign. She said she would exchange it for the sovereign she had just given the beggar. Sir George gave her the half-sovereign and she called after the beggar to stop and come back. The poor man wasn't too pleased about this. He had enough common sense to realise that no good was likely to come from any further contact with the gentry. Cautiously, he made his way back and stood before the couple, his eyes looking downwards.

To the utter surprise of both the rich and poor men, Lady Georgina said, 'Here, poor man, His Lordship desires to add a donation to my small gift.' She then gave the extra half-sovereign to the man. The beggar thanked her generosity, turned and ran as fast as his bare feet would carry him, so he could escape the wrath of His Lordship.

Lady Georgina merely smiled at her husband, linked his arm and continued their stroll. Sir George was speechless but that was the last time he ever tried to interfere with his wife's good works.

Sir George died in 1780 aged forty. Lady Georgina lived on until 1820, when she passed away in her seventy-first year.

REFERENCES

The Peerage and Baronetage of the British Empire, p.451, John Burke, London, 1845.

https://www.libraryireland.com/Pedigrees1/Forbes-2-Heremon.php

Historical Notes and Stories of the Co. Longford, pp.132–133, Farrell, Dollard, Dublin, 1886.

http://www.cracroftspeerage.Couk/online/content/granard1684.htm

35

SOME LONGFORD CHARACTERS

Every county produces its share of 'characters' – those individuals who stand out for one reason or another. The reasons are as varied as the characters themselves. Here are just three from Co. Longford.

JAMES REILLY'S' GUN

James Reilly, who was known as the 'Keenfellow', lived on the Drumhalry road that runs from Arva to Longford town. He was a thatcher by trade and during the Christmas season he added the trade of butcher for neighbouring farmers who had a fat cow to kill for Christmas. James died in 1890 in his eighty-sixth year. This story was collected by Patrick Duffy (73), a native of Drumhalry, who wrote it down in June 1930.

The failed Young Irelander Rebellion of 1848 happened when revolt was in the air throughout Europe and Ireland was still suffering from the throes of the Great Famine. The reaction of the English government was to confiscate all guns held by Catholic farmers.

On a certain night of that year, James Reilly was up late reading from *The Nation*, the nationalist weekly newspaper. Over his head above the fireplace there hung a gun. He was very proud of that gun and many stories abounded of his skill with the weapon. One evening as he stood in his doorway looking down towards the mountains, he saw a flock of geese flying towards his house.

He quickly rammed a large charge into the gun but did not have time to go out or remove the ramrod before the flock flew over his dwelling. He put the gun up the chimney and fired. He brought down six geese with that shot. The next day he went searching for the ramrod that had also been fired along with the shot. Eventually in the late evening he found the seventh goose pinned by the ramrod to a turf bank in Farrelly's bog nearby.

As Reilly sat quietly reading his newspaper, the tranquillity of the night was shattered when three men in disguise burst into the house. They took down his treasured gun and walked out. James could do nothing. He was prudent, and they didn't call him the Keenfellow for nothing.

Reilly was a very shrewd man and he told nobody including his family about the gun having been taken. A week passed and still the Keenfellow uttered not a word about it. On the eighth day the sergeant from Arva Barracks called at James' house with two of his men. The sergeant came straight to the point.

'Wasn't a gun taken from you and out of yer house lately?'

'Who told you that?' enquired James.

'Oh, we heard it going around,' said the sergeant.

'Where around, and who brought it round to you?' demanded James.

The sergeant answered gruffly, 'Now we heard it and isn't that lots. We also heard who it is that took the gun.'

James said nothing. The sergeant was determined to get the information he wanted. 'Wasn't it the "Plucker" that took out your gun? If you swear the charge against the "Plucker" we will have him arrested and you shall be well rewarded for swearing against him.'

'No,' said James, 'the "Plucker" never took my gun, it was you and those two other men with you who took it and before nightfall I shall swear that charge against you.'

The sergeant got into a frantic rage, shouting about what he could and would do to Reilly for being so daring and so impertinent as to accuse respectable officers of the law whose only purpose was to maintain peace and order in this disturbed country.

'From what I can prove against you,' said James, 'you are the real disturber and I'm not going to drop this serious charge easily.'

The sergeant and his men turned and went away muttering about reporting the matter to the District Inspector. The District Inspector (DI) in Arva at that time was a great sportsman, a fisher and a fowler. Anytime the DI was going through Drumhalry he would call on the Keenfellow for information about where a covey of game could be found.

On the day that James Reilly was going to make his charge against the sergeant, who should he meet but the DI on the road. The DI was on his way fowling. The two men fell into conversation about where he would find the best fowl. Soon the conversation turned to what the sergeant and his men had done.

Whatever was said between the Keenfellow and the District Inspector was never disclosed. That very night James Reilly's gun was shoved under his door. Attached carefully to the muzzle was a crisp new £5, a small fortune in the 1840s.

However, that was not the end of the dispute between the sergeant and the Keenfellow. As mentioned earlier, James Reilly was also a skilled butcher, a trade he only practised during the Christmas season. Up to that time in 1848, there were many strong farmers who killed their own fat cow or bullock for Christmas. All the near neighbours were given a part and the poor were not forgotten either.

As Christmas 1848 drew near, the Keenfellow bought himself a fat cow, killed her and set her carcass out on a grand stall at the Christmas Market. More to the point, he was underselling the town butcher by a penny a pound. The local butcher was very unhappy with this situation as he saw all his trade go to purchase parts of Reilly's cow.

The butcher headed straight for the sergeant in the barracks and complained that there was a man from the country selling 'fallen meat', that is meat from an animal that had died from disease. The sergeant went running to the market square, where he saw his great enemy standing beside his stall of beef. The immediate command from the 'arm of the law' was for the Keenfellow to clear out of the market with his 'fallen meat'. It was clear that failure to comply would result in the sergeant having it forcibly removed.

The Keenfellow obeyed without comment or protest. Before he left the town, he went with the man who had fattened the cow and from whom Reilly had lawfully purchased it and made a complaint about the whole affair to his friend, the District Inspector (DI). The advice given by the DI was, 'Go back with your cart of beef and throw it all down at the barrack's door. After that, "process" the sergeant for your loss and for damages.'

The process of the law awarded the Keenfellow three times the value of the cow and a decree was granted against the sergeant with a warning never to persevere in his own opinion without having legal proof about what was lawful or unlawful. This finally put an end to the conflict between James Reilly and the sergeant. It was true, the Keenfellow hadn't been given that nickname for nothing!

Pat Fee and 'Blessed Michael the Dark Angel'

This story was told to John Casey, Lanesboro, in November 2001 by Kitty Casey of Lismacmanus. Kitty in turn had been given the story by her late father, Simon Farrell.

Pat Fee was a Mayo man born in Killala around 1870. He came as a young boy with his mother to the Turlough in Rathcline parish. She often said that her husband was a soldier who had been killed in the wars. Mrs Fee was a 'street singer'. She performed normally at the fairs around Longford and Roscommon. The poor woman had a 'fondness for a drop' but on the positive side, it helped her singing greatly. If a neighbour were selling pigs or sheep at a fair, Mrs Fee was usually assured of a lift home in the crate (trailer). If she had drink taken, she would sing her heart out for the whole of the return journey.

Her neighbours built a hut for herself and her son up on the Commons. To survive, Mrs Fee had to beg for food. Sadly, she died in Longford Poorhouse and was buried in the graveyard there.

Her son, Pat, lived in the hut, which had a bottomless bucket as a chimney. He had no furniture except a stone to sit on and an armful of straw on which to sleep. As would be expected, he slept fully dressed. When the clothes got really dirty and needed to be washed, he would take them off and whack them against a rock. As he did so he used to say, 'That'll get the devilment out off ya!'

On Sundays, Pat would come out of the hut and face in the general direction of the chapel in Newtown. Around the time he thought the priest would be saying Mass he would pray himself. The poor man had a bit of a stammer and would say things like, 'Our Father who drafted into Heaven', 'Blessed Michael the Dark Angel', and 'Blessed Mary never virgin'. The late Fr Greene used to say that 'the man who made the offer was as good in God's eyes as the saints'.

Eventually Pat died, penniless. The neighbours, like good neighbours everywhere, looked after his burial. Michael Brennan's grandfather made him a coffin. On the night of the wake, the men had a gallon of porter for those who would stay the night. Lukey Farrell gave out the porter and a great number of people gathered in the little hut for the wake.

Unfortunately, Pat Fee had a hunched back and in order to lay him out they had to tie him down to a plank. As the wake progressed and the porter took hold, the wake games began. John Connor and one of the Concannons cut the rope and suddenly Pat sat up. Consternation broke out among the mourners and a general stampede for the door ensued. When the nerves settled the mourners returned, retied Pat to the plank and continued with the wake and polished off the porter. The following day, the late Pat's neighbours managed to get him 'boxed' into the coffin and carried the coffin to Cashel graveyard, where he was interred.

His tombstone reads:

Fee

Here lies Pat Fee of Turlough Fame

Who died 4th March 1900

Fr O'Farrell and the Young Policeman

During the 1870s, the parish priest of Killashee was Fr Richard O'Farrell, a direct descendant from the O'Farrells of Annaly. Fr O'Farrell, while a good and holy man, was often described as being very 'touchous'. This meant that if he felt he had ever been wronged in any way he was quick to punish any and all who he perceived as having been involved.

Fr O'Farrell loved the countryside. He especially loved to go fowling across the moors near where he ministered. Gun in hand, he would often be seen of an evening walking the roads looking for a good shot at any suitable fowl that rose.

One evening, as he walked along enjoying both the fresh air and the anticipation of a good shot, he met a young policeman new to the area. The policeman neither recognised the priest 'by sight nor by reputation'. At this time, the Coercion Act was in force in Ireland. Under this act anyone suspected on being involved in the Land War could be arrested and interred without trial.

The Coercion Act also forbade the carrying of guns except at certain hours of the day and then only with the owner in possession of a licence for the weapon. Fr O'Farrell was such an institution in the whole area that he would wander gun in hand day or night, never carrying a licence. The authorities never bothered him as it was known to all that he had no illegal intentions. This was not the case with the young new policeman.

The constable demanded that Fr O'Farrell stop, asked to see his licence and when no licence was forthcoming promptly arrested him under the Coercion Act and brought him back to the police barracks. He was detained in the dayroom of the station while the young policeman processed the paperwork necessary for the detention of the priest.

After Fr O'Farrell had been in the barracks for about an hour the sergeant came in and to his horror took in the scene at once. He ordered the policeman to immediately release the priest, which he did. The sergeant apologised for what had happened, explaining it was the young constable's inexperience and newness to the district that had led to this unfortunate situation.

The senior policeman finally managed to settle down the 'touchous' priest, who was irate at how he had been treated, especially as he was a man of the cloth. However, he refused to leave the barracks until the young policeman occupied the seat he had been sitting on while detained. There was a fine hot fire blazing in the hearth of the day room and while awaiting the novice, Fr O'Farrell moved the chair a good deal closer to the fire.

As soon as the constable sat on the chair, he became stuck to it and the chair became rooted to the floor. No matter how hard his colleagues tried, they were unable to move him. At that point, Fr O'Farrell left the barracks, leaving a hot and getting hotter recruit toasting by the blaze of the fire. The next morning the sergeant had to go the parish priest's house and beg him to release his by now very distressed constable.

Fr O'Farrell returned to the barracks, and the young policeman promised never to interfere nor arrest the priest if he was carrying his gun without a licence ever again.

REFERENCES

NFC 581, 162–168, James Reilly (85), Drumhalry Co. Longford. Collector: Patrick Duffy (74), Drumhalry, Co. Longford, June 1930.

John Casey, Gurtheengar, Lansboro, Co. Longford (unpublished).

Historical Notes and Stories of the Co. Longford, p.137, Farrell, Dollard, Dublin, 1886.